25 REASONS WHY SOME CHURCHES ARE NOT GROWING

—◊—

Dr. Marvin Scott, Ph.D.

PRESS

25 Reasons Why Small Churches Aren't Growing
by Dr. Marvin Scott, Ph.D.

Printed in the United States of America

ISBN 1-60034-700-2

www.xulonpress.com

25 REASONS WHY SOME CHURCHES ARE NOT GROWING

—◊◊◊—

DEDICATION

—ⱱⱱ—

This book is dedicated to pastors who are depressed because their churches are not growing. May this book assist you in your quest for church growth, especially those who feel like giving up.

INTRODUCTION

—〰—

This book addresses issues that will assist churches, whether they are large or small. In surveying, I have found that many of the problems that are in small churches also exist in large ones. It is possible for one church to grow in spite of its problems while another church with the same problems will not grow. For that reason I have provided a wide scope of information, leaving no stone unturned. I do promise you that this book will provide you with many things to ponder upon.

Each chapter has been carefully written to justify the purpose of this book. My primary purpose is to encourage everyone who reads it. Some chapters may seem redundant because some of them are closely related. It is my goal to build line by line and chapter upon chapter.

This book was also written with good intentions and not to attack anyone. Although this information will expose some, it is for the purpose of identifying and correcting problems in order that all may see the light. I am not without fault. A large portion of this book is a result of my mistakes. Many chapters are a diary of my first hand experiences and quest for church growth. I pray that my findings will save others from some of the pain that I have suffered as a pastor. I grew up with folks telling me that life experience is the best teacher. I have come to disagree with that statement. If you heed the instructions of others, you won't have to learn everything the hard way. You can save time, energy and money.

I don't have all the answers. I am busy seeking to improve my serve like everyone else. I pray that all who are striving to do the will of our Father will be blessed and win many souls into the kingdom because the harvest is truly great. May you receive a renewed measure of compassion for this generation.

"But when he saw the multitudes, he was moved with compassion on them, because they fainted, and were scattered abroad, as sheep having no shepherd. Then saith he unto his disciples, The harvest truly is plenteous, but the laborers are few; pray ye therefore the Lord of the harvest, that he will send forth laborers into his harvest."
(Matthew 9:36-38)

The Lord doesn't want anyone to perish, but that all may come to the knowledge of Him and be saved.

"The Lord is not slack concerning his promise, as some men count slackness; but is long-suffering to us-ward, not willing that any should perish, but that all should come to repentance." (2 Peter 3:9)

According to the census bureau, there are over six billion people in the world. That's enough people to pack out every church that exists and require each small church to become a large church. In all honesty we need more churches than those that already exist in order to accommodate the number of people who are in the world today. For that reason, may every large church get larger, every small church become large and may those whom God has called into the pastoral ministry get started.

Chapter twenty-six is a bonus chapter. It contains a wealth of knowledge, which has been written to let you see where we should be in this hour.

As you take your journey through this book, please keep in mind that pastoring is the greatest calling that one can enter into. May the anointing rest upon you as you serve God's people? Remember, the people that you serve are special to Him!

CHAPTER 1

OUTDATED PHILOSOPHY OF MINISTRY

—ᗰ—

"IN THE beginning God created the heaven and the earth.
And the earth was without form, and void; and darkness
was upon the face of the deep. And the spirit of God moved
upon the face of the waters." (Genesis 1:1-2)

From the very beginning of creation, God has been actively involved with changes. From the time we read "And the spirit of God moved on the face of the waters," you will find that changes took place daily.

One obvious problem with many small churches is that they have not changed their evangelistic approach to reach the unchurched. Nor have they improved their service to the attending congregation. We live in a high tech and sophisticated society, therefore the church needs to work smarter. People are motivated when they come to church and notice that the church is up with the times and is always improving on how it serves the people. In the secular world when people hear about a good sale or eat at a good restaurant, not only do they return, they tell others. They will do the same about their church when they are excited about changes and improvements.

It is time for small churches to come out of the old mindset of ministry. We do many things without giving it a second thought as to why we do what we do. A thoughtless church will unconsciously close many doors in the face of the unchurched. When a pastor starts a church, he/she needs to first sit down, and count up the cost by spending time seeking God for the vision of the newly formed ministry. Too many ministers are guilty of duplicating everything from their previous church when they start out. The structure of the foundation should be similar because there is but one gospel. You should be focused on why you were called. On the other hand, some ministers have thrown away the structure of the church of God. They have gone to the extreme copying ideas from everywhere until the ministry is operating without any authenticity. Every ministry should have its own uniqueness based upon the vision God has given it for the community it resides in. May God sensitize you to your purpose.

Some small churches have too many services on Sunday. They are in the building from morning until night, and it is the same group of people. The people need to go home and spend quality time with their families. They also need time to clean their homes and allow their kids freedom to play and unwind. That is one of the reasons why so many Christian families have the worst kids in school. "The handwriting is on the wall," you need to change your meeting time and eliminate those programs that are not working. For example, you may need to change bible study from Tuesday night to Wednesday night if most of your attendees have school-aged children and their school activities conflict with bible study.

If you have noticed that people are not coming out to weeknight services or if they are always leaving before the benediction, it is a sign that your services are too long. Weeknight bible studies should be limited to one hour or ninety minutes at the most. If you have the same few people testifying every week and all the kids know their testimonies by memory, that is not cute. It is sign that you are stuck in a rut, and you are wasting time.

A word of wisdom:

Before you start cutting out services, come up with a plan of action. Always introduce change in a positive manner. You may not need to eliminate testimony services al- together but you need to teach people what a testimony is and its purpose. Below are four examples of how testimonies can be shared:

1. As an opening at a men's or women's fellowship.
2. Have individuals share testimonies related to a partic- ular subject you are about to teach on as an example to enhance your sermon.
3. Before the worship leader starts singing , have a member from the evangelistic team or prayer team give a fiery report about the souls that were won to the Lord or the prayers that were answered during the week.
4. Have one or two special testimonies printed in the church bulletin on a weekly basis.

If you don't have enough experienced teachers for Sunday school and the program is not working, you need to seriously take a look at ways to build it up. Be aware that it is during Sunday school time or in the first 11 minutes of your morning worship when a visitor decides whether or not they are going to visit your church again.

As a pastor of a small church I highly recommend that you build up your Sunday school department because that may be the best you can do for now. Many large ministries have gotten to where they are today because of Sunday school. It has the potential to attract kids. Kids will pull in their parents, and kids also have a way of attracting other kids.

Don't tack on unnecessary services. Stick with those that are effective until the ministry creates a need for other programs. Don't waste your time doing something only because another church is doing it. There are churches that don't have Sunday school because it was not working for them. They tried many things to improve it and in all their efforts, it failed. They have other ways of educating the people such as:

1. Men's fellowship
2. Women's fellowship
3. Youth Ministry
4. Children's Church
5. Cell groups
6. Designated Conferences and Seminars
7. Bible classes or college

Many large churches have as much as five services on Sundays to accommodate the crowd. They have moved bible school and training classes to a weeknight.

21st Century pastoring:

It has been only a few years since we entered into this 21st century, and things are changing rapidly. This generation has been programmed by its surrounding. The need is very great. Jesus faced the same kinds of needs in his day. That is why he was moved with compassion, healing the sick and preaching the gospel.

"But when he saw the multitudes, he was moved with compassion on them, because they fainted, and were scattered abroad, as sheep having no shepherd."
(Matthew 9:36)

Jesus showed the people a lot of compassion because they were helpless. Please recognize the fact that this generation is crying out for help. They have good intentions , but they are weak. There is an abundance of grace flowing out of ministries who are operating out of compassion.

"And because iniquity shall abound, the love of many shall wax cold." (Matthew 24:12)

This society lacks the love our forefathers once knew. The above verse is saying because of sin the love we should have for God and His righteousness is gone. This problem has also slipped into the church. Now that we know what the problem is, it is up to us to pray and reinforce the love that should be in our congregation by teaching and demonstrating love.

The lost son:

"And when he came to himself, he said, How many hired servants of my father's have bread enough and to spare, and I perish with hunger! I will arise and go to my father, and will say unto him, Father, I have sinned against heaven, and before thee, And am no more worthy to be called thy son: make me as one of thy hired servants. And he arose, and came to his father. But when he was yet a great way off, his father saw him, and had compassion, and ran, and fell on his neck, and kissed him. And the son said unto him, Father, I have sinned against heaven, and before thee, And am no more worthy to be called thy son. But the father said to his servants, Bring forth the best robe, and put it on him; and put a ring on his hand, and shoes on his feet: And bring hither the fatted calf, and kill it; let us eat, and be merry: For this my son was dead, and is alive again; he was lost, and is found. And they began to be merry." (Luke 15:17-24)

The above scripture is an example of the ministry of reconciliation. The father in the story did not attack his son and say to him," I told you so." He had already instilled values in his son. He gave him space to grow up. The young son proved that he had a lot of growing to do. When he got out there, he met his match and he grew up very quickly. He returned home because of his father's reputation.

There are people that pastors have invested in who are considering returning back to church. Rebuking them won't be necessary because by the time they get back , they will be under conviction. Be prepared to restore them and watch out for the elder brother's spirit that maybe lurking in your congregation. They will criticize and condemn you for the way you handle the situation.

My main point in this chapter teaches that you must understand that the people of this generation are wiser in the earthly realm but not so in the spiritual realm (Luke 16:8). Don't assume that they know better when it comes to the standards set forth in the word of God. Spend time preparing wholesome sermons as you lead your congregation on the straight and narrow.

In the story with Gideon and the lost son, I shared the examples of the ministry of reconciliation. I personally believe that if you minister effectively to people , you will seldom need to admonish them about their shortcomings. They will fall under conviction and come to themselves. Conviction is the work of the Holy Spirit, which leads a person to godly sorrow.

CHAPTER 2

POOR MANAGEMENT SKILLS

A pastor should carry himself as an executive. You are the Chief Executive Officer (CEO) for your church. You may not necessarily have your hands in everything, but you are basically responsible for training and supervising people in the ways of righteousness. It is very challenging to train people who do not seem equipped for the job. It can also become tiring to work with a small group of people to bring to pass the vision that God has given you. It is recommended that pastors who have difficulty leading people get some outside help by taking a class in supervising or managing people. Most of the principles that apply in the secular world will apply in the church too. If you don't have time to attend classes at a school , you may consider reading some books from the business world on:

1. Managing people
2. How to reward employees
3. How to energize employees
4. Time management

You cannot walk around complaining that everybody is weak, and no one knows what to do.

"But if ye bite and devour one another, take heed that ye be not consumed one of another." (Galatians 5:15)

Pastors are called to pray and birth forth the ministry God has given to them. If you find yourself always disappointed by the people you serve, it is simply saying you have too many expectations of them and not enough expectation of God.

As a pastor you are going to see many problems in your church. Keep in mind; if you can recognize the problem, you must have faith for the solution.

There are times when you are to walk with the people. Most importantly, there are times when no one will see what you want him or her to see. When that happens, do as it says in the scripture below. "Go on before [ahead] of the people."

"And the Lord said unto Moses, Go on before the people, and take with thee of the elders of Israel; and they rod, wherewith thou smotest, take in thine hand, and go." (Exodus 17:5)

Don't attack the people for not seeing what you want them to see. Every problem you identify among your congregation should be something you should pray about. It is what you need to take charge over. You can ask God for the Spirit of understanding and gain from it. It is not a yoke to burden your self with.

A word of encouragement:

The main thing you want to watch out for is placing individuals who are loyal to you in charge. When they are in tune with the vision, they will properly represent you in your absence.

It is not too late for you. The following examples reveal that God can take the worst cases and turn them into miracles.

He did it for Gideon:

"And the Lord said unto Gideon, By the three hundred men that lapped will I save you, and deliver the Midianites into thine hand: and let all the other people go every man unto his place." (Judges 7:7)

First of all, Gideon did not feel equipped to do the job. After God convinced him that he was chosen, God tested the people that were with him. God reduced the number from 32,000 to only three hundred men. It did not seem logical for a small group because the enemies' number was so large that they could not be counted. The story ended with Gideon and his men winning the battle because the Lord was with them. The key to success is obeying God at all times.

He did it for the four lepers:

"And they rose up in the twilight to go unto the camp of the Syrians: and when they were come to the uttermost part of the camp of Syria, behold, there was no man there." (2King 7:5)

In this story God used men that people had cast out of the city because they were unclean. It was because of their determination that God used them to find the food that He had spoken of through the prophet the day before. God will use people that others have considered least likely to succeed to bring to pass His will on the earth.

David and his men did it:

"But David pursued, he and four hundred men: for two hundred abode behind, which were so faint that they could not go over the book Besor." (1 Samuel 30:10)

David pursued his enemy and recovered all because God told him to pursue. Any time God tells you to do something, it matters not who is with you, who leaves or who gets tired along the way. You are going to recover everything that the enemy has stolen from you because God's word never fails.

In ministry, it is required that you recognize what is needed in your church and take it to where it needs to go. You may have a church full of people that are weak and unskillful. At the same time you may notice another pastor who has a church of professionals. Although your church may require more than that of your colleagues, don't cut it down. Roll up your sleeves and get to work.

"Then said he unto the dresser of his vineyard, Behold, these three years I come seeking fruit on this fig tree, and find none: cut it down; why cumbereth in the ground? And he answering said unto him, Lord, let it alone this year also, till I shall dig about I, and dung it: and if it bear fruit, well: and if not, then after that thou shalt cut it down."
(Luke 13:7-9)

For those who consider their church is a hopeless case and will never come to anything, think on the following scriptures:

"But God has chosen the foolish things of the world to confound the wise; and God hath chosen the weak things of the world to confound the things which are mighty; And base things of the world, and things which are despised,

hath God chosen, yea, and things which are not,
to bring to nought things that are: That no flesh should
glory in his presence." (1 Corinthians 1:27-29)

"Beat your plowshares into swords, and your pruninghooks
into spears; let the weak say, I am strong." (Joel 3:10)

You are not an all-around pastor ("A Jack of All Trades")

If you hear people referring to you as the above, think again because you are:

1. Setting you self up for becoming burned-out.
2. Doing too much.
3. Shortening your life.
4. Controlling and stifling the growth of the church.

Before I go on, I must interject the fact that becoming burned-out is the number one reason why many pastors become discouraged and fall into sin. Ministry is a vocation, and it is very demanding on one's well being; therefore, a large percentage of our fulfillment comes out of it and if you don't get the proper fulfillment out of it, there is a tendency to seek it in all the wrong places.

Learn to delegate authority. That is the mark of being a good leader. You must teach others to do what you can do. Get away from doing minor tasks, and assign them to others. That will free your mind, body and soul for more things that God has called you to do.

"But we will give ourselves continually to prayer,
and to the ministry of the word." (Acts 6:4)

There is a mandate for you to move into a higher level of ministry. We are in the last days,and there are certain scriptures that reveal that we need to take responsibility for the spiritual deficit in the world. Please note I said take the responsibility and not the blame. It is no time to point fingers, but you must recognize that people are guilty not because they are willfully wicked. They are weak and vulnerable. They are not prepared for the things coming upon the earth. As a pastor, you must move in the power of God and know that you are in demand; however, there is a price to pay to fulfill this call. Arm yourself so you can take your stand and break through the barrier that seems impossible to break. It is only the initial breaking that seems hard. Once you get through the first stage, it will become easier. The following verse reveals to us that we must [die] suffer to bring forth much fruit.

"Verily, verily, I say unto you, Except a corn of wheat fall into the ground and die, it abideth alone: but if it die, it bringeth forth much fruit." (John 12:24)

You are on the brink of a great move of God. Rise up over your flesh and move in the power of the Holy Ghost because you have been equipped by God Almighty.

"But ye shall receive power, after that the Holy Ghost is come upon you: and ye shall be witnesses unto me both in Jerusalem and in all Judea, and in Samaria, and unto the uttermost part of the earth." (Acts 1:8)

The following scriptures identify what happened in the days of old and what we are dealing with today.

"And Gideon said unto him, Oh my Lord, if the Lord be with us, why then is all this befallen us? And where be

*all his miracles which our fathers told us of, saying, Did
not the Lord bring us up from Egypt? But the Lord hath
forsaken us, and delivered us into the hands
of the Midianites." (Judges 6:13)*

Gideon was a victim. He did not know where the fault lay;
therefore, he accused the Lord of forsaking him. Of course
he was wrong because God will never forsake us. With the
proper guidance he was led to trust God. The angel that came
to Gideon did not rebuke him but instead he ministered unto
him. Please provide your flock with clarity in your preaching
and teaching so they can walk with God without stumbling.
People don't have the tolerance for hell-fire and brimstone
sermons if they are not offered solutions. The churches
of yesteryears were good at identifying the problems but
provided no answers. This generation is saying "don't attack
me for being in the hole; provide me with instructions how
to get out or how to avoid the next one.

*"In those days there was no king in Israel: every man did
that which was right in his own eyes." (Judges 21:25)*

As a pastor your patience are going to be stretched
more than ever before because people have been wrongly
programmed by society. This generation does whatever
seems right in their own eyes.

CHAPTER 3

UNAWARE OF THE POTENTIAL OF THE MEMBERS OF YOUR CONGREGATION

—ɷ—

Ministry gifts:

Every one is not going to show up with their lives in perfect order. Some of them are going to require a lot of work. In those cases, you must have faith in the people because it is God who performs miracles. It is your responsibility to become knowledgeable of all ministry gifts and provide the people with the proper training. It is also your job to bring out the best in the people that are in your church. You are their servant. Your primary objective is to get the people involved with the Ministry Of Helps. It means exactly what it says **helps**. As Jesus called his disciples, he gave them things to do. He was there to coach and train them. He tested them on many occasions. For example , he tested Philip to see what he was going to do about feeding the multitude. Jesus already had in mind what he was going to do (John 6:6). Jesus was careful to see what was on their minds. He always allowed them to share in organizing the crowd when he got ready to serve them. By the time the disciples received the

Holy Spirit in Acts chapter two, Jesus had already exposed them to the Ministry of Helps. From their prior experiences they knew how to mobilize the early church after Pentecost.

I am not a prophet, but I am not limited to its operating. I am the shepherd of the house and every ministry gift is subject to me. Therefore, I am familiar with the working of them all. I have learned about them by carefully studying them in college and exposing my self to them first hand by inviting various ministries in, or attending various conferences such as:

1. Pastors and Leadership Conferences
2. World Evangelism Conferences
3. Inner City Evangelism Conferences
4. Foreign Ministry Training Seminars
5. Deliverance Ministry Conferences
6. Youth Conferences
7. Ministry Gifts
8. Music and Worship Conferences
9. Healing School
10. School of the Prophets
11. Cell Ministry Conferences

Resumes:

When a new member fills out an application to become a member of our church, I request a resume from them. That gives us some extra information about the person, and we use that information to get them involved because people come with experiences that we need to be aware of. Look at the following scripture about the man that Jesus declared had the greatest faith in all Israel. He possessed this type of faith because he used it daily in the work place.

"For I also am a man set under authority, having under me soldiers, and I say unto one, Go, and he goeth; and to another, Come, and he cometh; and to my servants, Do this, and he doeth it. When Jesus heard these things, he marvelled at him, and turned him about, and said unto the people that followed him, I say unto you, I have not found so great faith, no, not in Israel." (St. Luke 7:8-9)

When you notice individuals in your congregation who have a passion for something , that is an indication that you need to assign them to something closely related to their interest to get them involved. Remember if they have the ability to notice a need or a problem, they will make a good problem solver.

The individuals that are heading the following programs in my church had a passion for it and I got them involved it.

1. Prayer team
2. Outreach team
3. Fund raising team
4. Youth involvement
5. Men's ministry
6. Women's ministry
7. Singing groups
8. Sound equipment
9. Sunday School Superintendent
10. Finance Committee

Once these individuals proved themselves faithful, I assigned the most aggressive one as the team leader. Now that I have my team leaders in place, I meet with them monthly. They are my staff. They are the people that I make sure stay motivated and have a clear understanding of the church's vision.

Get the people healed:

When a person joins the church, they normally come with a need. It is our job to get them healed if they are physically or spiritually sick. Exposing them to what God can do is how you handle this. It is not hard to get people programmed to becoming miracle minded.

People grow in stages. That is why I heavily stress getting them involved. It is through accomplishments that they gain confidence, and when their confidence level is high, they will defeat personal struggles.

*"Wherefore, my beloved, as ye have always obeyed, not as in my presence only, but now much more in my absence, **work** out your own salvation with fear and trembling."*
(Philippians 2:12)

The people need to feel good about their church

An alarming number of people don't feel good about their Church. That is why they don't invite people out. Some people come to church with low self-esteem and other related hang-ups. They need coaching and motivation to make them feel like they are somebody. Once you replace the negative with the positive, keep them motivated by including them in what is going on in the church. Never over look people, leaving them with the impression that you already have enough help. When a person has an idea or suggestion, hear them out. It's a good idea to encourage your staff to back you as you work with newcomers. Your staff and older members can be your worst enemies when new members want to participate. If a new member comes up with ways to generate funds and it has potential, work with it and make sure that it does not fall through the cracks. New members also have energy and ideas for out-reach programs, but more than likely they may not know all the pitfalls. Share with them in a positive manner how to put the program over. What I am saying is, whatever you do; don't ever let a member's project fall through the cracks as a method of teaching them a lesson. You will better serve them by sharing why something won't work and then come up with an alternative. Never close a door on someone's excitement without opening another door.

The days of the one-man show is over. Every member has been divinely placed in your church for a purpose. Seek out their potential and allow them to fulfill their destiny.

CHAPTER 4

NO VISION

—◊◊◊—

This chapter deals with the fact that some ministries are failing miserably because they have no vision. You must get focused and stay focused on what God has said regardless to what comes against your vision. You cannot change every time you are faced with a dilemma. When things go wrong, remember who you are in Christ and what he said to you when the vision was fresh. When God says something, He is not going to change His mind. When Moses and the Children of Israel got to the Red Sea, there was no place to go. It was not for them to seek God for a new direction. It was another opportunity for Moses to use the rod and see the salvation of the Lord. Through the Red Sea was the route for them to take. The sea only proved to be an enemy to those that rose up against them.

On several occasions I had the privilege of sitting under the ministry of the Late Kenneth E. Hagins and I read his book entitles *"Purpose, Pursuit and Plan."* That book teaches on the importance of praying the vision into reality because we serve a powerful God. I highly recommend this book to every pastor.

What is a Vision?

A vision is the ability to perceive, discern and anticipate; to have foresight and to use one's imagination.

The Ability to Perceive:

If it is a vision that God has initiated, it should not be based upon your strength or ability to do it alone. It should be based upon the Holy Spirit working in your life to bring it to pass. Once you perceive that God has given a vision , it becomes your responsibility to guard your mind so that nothing takes it away from you.

The Ability to Discern:

The ability to discern is a step higher than perceiving. When you perceive something, it is basically the unveiling of a vision and at that stage there is a lot of excitement. It is an exciting time because your emotions and adrenaline are flowing. Discernment is the ability to apply the wisdom that is necessary to keep you going when the excitement begins to wear off. When discernment is at work, you start separating and dividing things because it is through your experience that you stay motivated when bad news comes. Lastly, a discerning person will stick to the task when others would have given up.

The Ability to Anticipate:

You should compile a journal and document everything you do. It is through your accomplishments that you will stay strong. When it seems like something is not working, I advise you to trust God to do what he has promised to you. Your faith is only being put to the test. As you continue to apply the faith, you will see it as an opportunity to experience more of God's power. It is a part of the plan for your works to be tried by fire. Instead of whining and complaining, anticipate the victory.

The Ability to Have a Foresight:

Through faith and discipline you should develop a keen sense of knowledge for the plan of God that He has introduced to you. When there is nothing tangible to look at, you must stop basing things upon what you see. Because of foresight and foreknowledge you should base it upon what you know.

The Ability to Imagine:

If you abide in Him and His words abide you, you will discover that God will use your imagination above measure. You must keep your mind in tune with the things of God so that the devil doesn't trick you into coming up with the wrong interpretation of a vision. You must stay ahead of him with understanding so that every time he tries to deceive or attempts to discourage you, you will be anchored in God's plan. Jesus was in tuned with his Father. Every scheme of his enemies was put to silence. The devil will be no match for you when you are where you are supposed to be.

The Process:

When God called you to start your church with the calling, He gave you a vision and with the vision came the anointing to operate in the gift in order for it to come to pass. The anointing enables you to do those things that seem impossible.

Like Joshua, we are called to build upon a foundation that is already laid. The vision was first given to Moses. They were called to return to the land of their forefathers and repossess it. In the scripture below I have shared some insights.

*"NOW after the death of Moses the servant of the Lord it came to pass, that the Lord spake unto Joshua the son of Nun, Moses' minister, saying, **Moses my servant is dead;** now therefore arise, go over this Jordan, thou, and all this people, unto a land which I do give to them, even to the children of Israel. Every place that the sole of your foot shall tread upon, that have I given unto you, as I said unto Moses. From the wilderness and this Lebanon even unto the great river, the river Euphrates, all the land of the Hittites, and unto the great sea toward the going down of the sun, shall be your coast. There shall not any man be able to stand before thee all the days of thy life: as I was with Moses, so I will be with thee: I will not fail thee, nor forsake thee, Be strong and of a good courage: for unto this people shalt thou divide for an inheritance the land, which I sware unto their fathers to give them. Only be thou strong and very courageous, that thou mayest observe to do according to all the law, which Moses my servant commanded thee: turn not from it to the right hand or to the left, that thou mayest prosper whithersover thou goest. This book of the law shall not depart out of thy mouth; but thou shalt meditate therein day and night, that thou shalt make thy way prosperous, and then thou shalt have good success. Have I not commanded you? **Be strong and very courageous.** Do not be **terrified**; do not be **discouraged**, for the Lord your God will be with you wherever you go."*
(Joshua 1:1-9)

Points to Ponder:

1. Moses is dead.
2. Command – Don't forget; don't lose the urgency.
3. Strong and courageous – The ability to walk alone.
4. Terrified (do the opposite) – Bold and very aggressive
5. Discouraged (do the opposite) – Encouraged and highly motivated

Moses is Dead:

Moses' death represented change. It was not meant for the people to abandon the vision, however it meant for them recognize that God had brought them as far as Moses was allowed to take them. The foundation of their vision remained. They were still supposed to focus on the Promise Land. The only change that they should have experienced was the style of leadership. It was up to Joshua to take them across the Jordan and into the Promised Land. The foundation of the vision remained. They were still supposed to focus on the Promised Land. Moses' death only represented the changing of the guards. They were only to memorialize Moses for thirty days and move on.

I have been around people who are still memorializing a pastor and the person has been deceased for many years. When you get into a lengthy ritual of memorializing a person, it is a form of idol worship. It will stop the growth of the ministry. You will have those that will walk around and say, *"Nothing is supposed to change."* If it were the will of God for nothing to change, the person would not have died. There are times when a pastor dies in the process of a church pursuing a vision. When that takes place, the group must go on and realize that the new leader that God will raise up is not in competition with the fallen pastor , but it is up to them to take the church on to the next level. Some things will change because God doesn't deal with leaders the same way . The congregation must be flexible. It is a new order and any change that occurs will cause the church to grow. If it is a change in the time of the service or changing bible study from Wednesday night to Tuesday night to accommodate the people , that is nothing to fight over. If the new minister starts preaching and teaching a doctrine that is not in line with the bible and tries to undermine what the church stood for, then that is something to resist. If that is the case, the congregation should seek to restore the correct doctrine so that the church does not get out of the will of God.

Command:

They were commanded because God did not want them to forget what he said to them. When it seemed like the job was impossible to accomplish, God reminded them all over again about the original promise. They were not to lose the urgency of what was said to them. If they had not lost the urgency, they would not have become weary and started complaining along the way. Lastly, they were informed about what course they should take. It is important to pay close attention what God says because the enemy will offer a counterfeit and persuade you to go in the wrong direction. Keep in mind there is no easier route. You must stay the course regardless of the suffering. You can lose focus by watching another church that seems to be moving faster than you.

Strong and Courageous:

Pastoral ministry is the loneliest of all ministry gifts. Many pastors give up because it is not every day you will have some one to talk and walk with you from one test to the next. For that reason , many will think that they are the only one doing what they are doing. Loneliness caused Elijah to go into isolation.

"But he himself [alone] went a day's journey into the wilderness, and came and sat down under a juniper tree: and he requested for himself that he might die; and said, It is enough; now, O Lord, take away my life; for I am not better than my fathers." (1 Kings 19:4)

While Elijah was having a pity party, God was still blessing the other prophets. The problem was that he had isolated himself from the rest of God's people. He was in the wrong place seeking to be encouraged. God had to remind him that he was not the only prophet left.

"Yet I have left me seven thousand in Israel, all the knee which have not bowed unto Baal, and every mouth which hath not kissed him." (1 Kings 19:18)

Terrified:

They were commanded not to become terrified because there were giants in the land. The complete opposite of being terrified is to become bold and very aggressive. The enemy seeks to shut down the people of God by getting them to watch the problem and lose sight on God. You must stand your ground and know that "no weapon that is formed against you shall prosper."

Discouraged:

To ensure that you don't become discouraged in the midst of doing God's will, you must stay positive, encourage your self and stay highly motivated. You are not to be moved by your emotions or the words of doubters. You should only be moved by the word of the Lord.

Know This:

1. A vision does not make sense to the observer. You have to trust and believe in your vision when the devil tells you; "You are a fool for believing in it".
2. You don't have the ability to bring a vision to pass, but God does.
3. Your staff must be joined to you the leader and not the people.

Everyone will not understand all parts of the vision:

"AND Jacob dwelt in the land wherein his father was a stranger, in the land of Canaan. These are the generations of Jacob. Joseph, being seventeen years old, was feeding the flock with his brethren; and the lad was with the sons of Bilhah, and with the sons of Zilpah, his father's wives: and Joseph brought unto his father their evil report. Now Israel loved Joseph more than all his children, because he was the son of his old age: and he made him a coat of many colours. And when his brethren saw that their father loved him more than all his brethren, they hated him, and could not speak peaceably unto him. And Joseph dreamed a dream, and he told it his brethren: and they hated him yet the more. And he said unto them, Hear, I pray you, this dream which I have dreamed: For, behold, we were binding sheaves in the field, and, lo, my sheaf arose, and also stood upright; and, behold, your sheaves stood around about, and made obeisance to my sheaf. And his brethren said to him, Shalt thou indeed reign over us? Or shalt thou indeed have dominion over us? And they hated him yet the more for his dreams and for his words. And he dreamed yet another

dream, and told it his brethren, and said, Behold, I have dreamed a dream more; and, behold, the sun the moon and the eleven stars made obeisance to me. And he told it to his father, and to his brethren: and his father rebuked him, and said unto him, What is this dream that thou hast dreamed? Shall I and thy mother and thy brethren indeed come to bow down ourselves to thee to the earth? And his brethren envied him; but his father observed the saying."
(Genesis 37:1-11)

Joseph saw exactly what was going to happen to him and his family. His family understood the dream, but they did not want to accept the fact that God had chosen him to rule over them. Instead of appreciating him and thanking God for putting a gifted person in their midst, they became jealous of him and attacked him. In spite of his brothers hating him, Joseph would not stop talking about where he was going nor did he stop dreaming. Little did they know that they assisted Joseph in going to the place where his dreams would come to pass and benefit the world. It was not in his father's house that the dream had any significance. Joseph maintained his relationship with God in spite of his troubles. Because of his faith, everything eventually came together.

"AND all the congregation of the children of Israel jour-neyed from the wilderness of Sin, after their journeys, according to the commandment of the Lord, and pitched in Rephidim: and there was no water for the people to drink. Wherefore the people did chide with Moses, and said, Give us water that we may drink. And Moses said unto them, Why chide ye with me? wherefore do ye tempt the Lord? And the people thirsted there for water; and the people murmured against Moses, and said, wherefore is this that thou hast brought us up out of Egypt, to kill us and our children and our cattle with thirst? And Moses cried unto

43

the Lord, saying, What shall I do unto this people?
they be ready to stone me. And the Lord said unto Moses,
Go on before the people, and take with thee of the elders of
Israel; and thy rod, wherewith thou smothest the river,
take in thine hand, and go." (Exodus 17:1-5)

The people followed Moses based upon what they saw. They never reached the place where they trusted God based upon His reputation. From one miracle to the next they should have learned that God is not a man that He should lie.

You are an Original:

The bible is like a recipe book. If you follow the instructions, it will come out all right. You can be in Virginia and some else can be in California, but if both follow the same recipe for an apple pie, although you may differ because of your experience, personality and environment , when it is all said and done, both of you will have an apple pie. The same applies with what you are doing in your church verses another pastor in his/her church. Although you will have your own uniqueness and differences, overall it will be a church of God if you follow the same rule set forth in the word of God. Get out of the habit of always wanting to copy something off of someone else. I am not saying you don't need others, but I am saying don't go over board in looking to others rather than seeking God for your self. When you are too dependent on others, you will lose sight of your vision and God's ability to do what He has promised.

I end this chapter with a final word from Habakkuk:

"And the Lord answered me, and said, Write the vision, and
make it plain upon tables, the he may run that readeth it.
For the vision is yet for an appointed time, but at the end it

shall speak, and not lie: though it tarry, wait for it; because it will surely come, it will not tarry." (Habakkuk 2:2-3)

CHAPTER 5

OUT OF TOUCH WITH THE COMMUNITY

—m—

If there are disputes and problems with the people in the community where your church resides such as parking or too much noise coming from your services, seek to resolve it as quickly as possible. You don't want to be in a neighborhood and your members are not getting along with the people because of an ongoing feud. You must pray that God give you favor with your neighbors, because above all else, you should be there as a light to the community.

If you are dealing with individuals who are unreasonable, you are dealing with a spirit. In that case you are under a spiritual attack. When under attack , you should engage in warfare praying which includes fasting.

A church can be out of touch with a community from a natural perspective as well as from a spiritual perspective.

Natural perspective:

Ministries are moving in communities because of affordability rather than for the purpose of evangelism. Once you arrive in a community, you should seek to take advantage of every opportunity to spread the gospel. If any of these needs are present where your church resides, seek God to open a door for you to get involved in one or more of the following areas.

1. Homelessness
2. Crime and substance abuse
3. Tutoring and Literacy program
4. Unemployment.
5. Teen's pregnancy
6. Poverty
7. Unattended children

It also necessary to build a relationship with the people and become knowledgeable of what's going on in the neighborhood such as:

1. When there is death in a family.
2. The birth of a baby.
3. New residents.
4. Those who have a loved one who is sick.
5. Those laid-off from work.
6. Weddings
7. Graduations.
8. Retirements

One might say how are we going to find out what's happening with people in a community? I would like to suggest that you pray for the community daily. The next you thing you should do is ride around the neighborhood in your free time. As you ride something will possibly spark your interest. If you are ever invited to something in the community makes it your business to go because that is your crack in the door. Please observe the following scripture:

"AND the third day there was a marriage in Cana of Galilee; and the mother of Jesus was there: And both Jesus was called, and his disciples, to the marriage. And when they wanted wine, the mother of Jesus saith unto him, they have no wine." (John 2:1-3)

Mary got involved when it she found out about the problem at the wedding. We must do the same when we are in a neighborhood. Mary was not quick to give up. Her determination caused a miracle to happen.

If they don't invite you, you should consider reaching out to them in one or more of the following ways:

1. Host a block party.
2. Host a community day including a health and job fair.
3. Hold a vacation bible school.
4. Start a mentoring program.
5. Send out Christmas cards.
6. Send out flyers announcing major events.
7. Advertise in the local community news.
8. Get on the community mailing list if they have one.
9. Have a family and friends day.
10. Host a "back to school bash"
11. Have someone to represent your church at the PTA meetings at the school in the community.

Spiritual Perspective:

When it comes to the spiritual side of the ministering to the community, you must realize that you are not wrestling against flesh and blood but against spiritual wickedness in high places (Ephesians 6:12). There is such a thing as *territorial spirits* fighting against the church. That's why pastors and their congregations need to fast and pray about the location they hold services in. Some areas are worse than others are when it comes to the level of principalities. You may attend a Leadership or Church Growth Conference. After it's over you will return home excited about implementing all kinds of programs you learned about but it all failed. It is possible that you did not take time to consider what you are up against in your neighborhood. For that reason you need to research the area and find out as much history as you can. Most of this information can be found in the local library along with all the statistics on the people in the city. Once you come across information, have your congregation join you in a season of fasting and praying against those forces. Pull them down in the name of Jesus. You may be holding service in a building or on a property that was once used for worshipping false gods. If that is the case, there is a good chance that there are forces that are hindering what you are trying to accomplish.

Moses and Joshua sent out spies so that they could have information on what they were dealing with. Please note the following:

Moses' Spies:

"And Moses sent them to spy out the land of Canaan, and said unto them, Get you up this way southward, and go up into the mountain: And see the land, what it is; and the people that dwelleth therein, whether they be strong or weak, few or many; And what the land is that they dwell in, whether it be good or bad; and what cities they be that they dwell in, whether in tents, or in strong holds; And what the land is, whether it be fat or lean, whether there be wood therein or not. And be ye of good courage, and bring of the fruit of the land. Now the times was the time of the firstripe grapes." (Numbers 13:17-20)

The majority of the spies were fearful. They sentenced the children of Israel to 40 years in the wilderness by the words of their mouths.

Joshua's Spies:

"AND Joshua the son of Nun sent out of Shittim two men to spy secretly, saying, Go view the land, even Jericho. And they went, and come into an harlot's house, name Rahab, and lodged there." (Joshua 2:1)

The courage of the two spies motivated the Israelites to quickly mobilize themselves and capture Jericho.

In the Old Testament the people fought against nations to take possession of the land. Today, we engage in spiritual warfare by praying and pulling down the strongholds of the enemy. We are to take authority over forces that are holding a person in captivity or are controlling territories (2 Corinthians 10:3-6).

CHAPTER 6

SELF-DRIVEN

—ɷ—

This chapter deals with how to be Spirit-led instead of being self-driven. Under the topic of being Spirit-led, I have chosen Jesus as an example and under the topic of being self-driven, I chose Samson as an example. Although the Spirit came upon Samson on many occasions to defeat the enemy, Samson was basically a self-driven person, which led to his demise. As you follow along, you will see that my two choices clearly drive my point home.

Due to the fact that pastoring calls for making a large amount of decisions, one can easily fall into being self-driven. To be led by the spirit requires much time in prayer and mediation. We live in a time when everyone is pressed for time; therefore, we have the tendency to cut corners and not be led by the spirit. Keep in mind, in order to please the Father you must do it His way. This explains why so many get into being self-driven. Satan will deceive you into thinking that you can obtain faster results by cutting corners. Cutting corners only takes the focus off of God and places it upon man's ability.

Jesus:

Jesus was very powerful when he walked the earth. He often spoke about pleasing the Father. He did not come to do his will, but to do the will of Him that sent him (John 4:34). The greatest test in this hour is to use self-control and not conform to your surrounding but to control your surroundings through the power of the Holy Spirit.

The Sequence to Jesus' Power:

"Then was Jesus led up of the Spirit into the wilderness to be tempted of the devil." (Matthew 4:1)

Jesus spent time preparing himself before he entered into public ministry. The devil never stood a chance because Jesus stayed ahead of him at all times. When Satan showed up in the wilderness, Jesus had already accomplished 40 days of fasting and building himself up spiritually. The scripture says, "And whosoever doth not bear his cross, and come after me, cannot be my disciple" (Luke 14:27) It is noted that Jesus taught his disciples how to become great followers of God; he was their perfect example.

"And when he had sent the multitude away, he went up into a mountain apart to pray; and when the evening was come, he was there alone." (Matthew 14:23)

No matter what Jesus accomplished in a day, he did not become carried away with his accomplishments and not prepare himself for the next assignment. The enemy of your next victory could be your past accomplishments.

*"Then cometh Jesus with them unto a place called
Gethsemane and saith unto the disciples, Sit ye here,
while I go and pray yonder." (Matthew 26:36)*

When Jesus was about to face the greatest test of his life,
he prayed until he received his break through. Jesus never
lost the urgency to stay the course and finish his assignment
before dying on the cross.

*"And it came to pass in those days, that he went out
into a mountain to pray, and continued all night
in prayer to God." (Luke 6:12)*

As repetitious as these scriptures may seem, it is not the
same story. It is merely pointing out that Jesus was consis-
tent in how he behaved himself in this world. It also teaches
that our strength comes from staying close to the Lord. The
devil will tempt you to slack up on your prayer life and to get
busy trying to fix things on your own. It won't get done like
that. God's way is the best way.

*"And it came to pass about an eight days after these
sayings, he took Peter and John and James, and went up
into a mountain to pray. And as he prayed, the fashion
of his countenance was altered, and his raiment was
white and glistering." (Luke 9:28-29)*

Jesus exposed Peter, James and John, who eventually
became the leading Apostles, to things to come. There will
never be a time when God is not revealing to His church what
He is about to do. We must prevail in the things of God until
we get beyond those things of the flesh that will easily trip us
up. God is not worrying over what you are worried about. He
rules and every form of authority is under his control. You

must pray until you break through the barriers of your will into the supernatural realm.

"But Jesus did not commit himself unto them, because he knew all men, And needed not that any should testify of man: for he knew what was in man." (John 2:24-25)

In the gospel of John you will find that Jesus was very accurate in every thing he did and he would not allow any situation or anybody to stand in his way. He went nowhere ahead of schedule, nor did he stay anywhere longer than his schedule allowed.

"And this he said to prove him: for he himself knew what he would do." (John 6:6)

When he ministered to his disciples, to the crowds or dealt with his opponents, he knew what he was going to do. The Spirit led him at all times and he had the ability to discern what to do about every situation he faced.

Samson:

Samson was definitely raised up by God to be a judge over His people. The enemy of his day was determined to keep God's people in bondage; therefore, Samson's job was not an easy one. Because the Philistines were a cunning group of people, Samson needed to maintain a strong relationship with God in order to stay ahead of them at all times. As you read along you will see how he lived in violation of the instruction given to his parents by the angel. He did not follow complete instructions. That explains why he became self-driven, and slowly but surely, he was brought down.

The Sequence of Samson's Failure:

Samson had no choice but to fight on various occasions, but he also had the responsibility of cleansing himself after touching unclean things as prescribed in the book of Numbers chapter 6 because he was a Nazarite. He also had a habit of not telling his parents what he had done, which revealed that he wanted to do his own thing. If he had revealed to them what he was doing, they would have ensured that he kept the vow of being a Nazarite by offering the proper sacrifice and engaging in the ceremonial cleansing necessary to maintain his strength. Samson spent no time in prayer. He took the Spirit of God for granted. When the Spirit eventually departed from him, he was the last to know (Judges 16:20). Below I have noted the unclean things that he touched and never sought cleansing after handling them.

*"Then went Samson down, and his father and his mother, to Timnath and came to the vineyards of Timnath: and behold, a **young lion** roared against him. And the Spirit of the Lord came mightily upon him, and he rent him as he would have rent a kid, and he had nothing in his hand: but he told not his father or his mother what he had done."*
(Judges 14:5-6)

*"And after a time he returned to take her, and he turned aside to see the **carcase of the lion:** and, behold, there was a swarm of bees and honey in the carcase of the lion. And he took thereof in his hands, and went on eating, and came to his father and mother, and he gave them, and they did eat: but he told not them that he had taken the honey out of the carcase of the lion." (Judges 14:8-9)*

*"And Samson went and caught three hundred **foxes,** and took firebands, and turned tail to tail, and put a fireband in the midst between two tails." (Judges 15:4)*

*"And he found a new **jawbone of an ass**, and put forth his hand, and took it and slew a thousand men therewith. And Samson said, With the jawbone of an ass, heaps upon heaps, with the jaw of an ass have I slain a thousand men." (Judges 15:15-16)*

Samson eventually was captured solely because he relied on his might and his power. It is true that God gives us strength but at the same time we are supposed to rely upon Him. The following scripture admonishes us about trusting in our own strength.

"Then he answered and spake unto me, saying, This is the word of the Lord unto Zerubbabel, saying, Not by might, nor by power, but by my spirit, saith the Lord of hosts." (Zechariah 4:6)

When you take matters into your own hands, you are operating in your own might and power, trying to accomplish the will of God. When you take your hands out of it and allow God to fight the battle, is when the Spirit can accomplish the work.

CHAPTER 7

OVERLY CAUTIOUS

—⅏—

If you are a negative thinking person and easily intimidated, there is a good possibility that you are your own worst enemy. Secondly, if you find yourself thinking that most pastors who lead large churches are arrogant and full of pride, think again, they may only be outgoing and not afraid of challenges. If that is the case, they are acting like you should act. Pastors are supposed be God-fearing, but not to the point where they are inferior to others. Overly cautious people are usually restless and full of suspicion. When a person is like that, it is a form of bondage. I have expounded further on this matter under the topic of insecurity as I discuss David and Eliab.

Some pastors are so afraid that they will operate in the flesh that they are literally in the flesh trying to control themselves. It is actually the godly ambition and aggressiveness that God has placed in them that's trying to come forth. This chapter teaches you how to overcome being a timid Christian so that you can take authority and reach masses of people.

There is a process to overcoming being overly cautious. The process consists of putting pressure on those things that you are uncomfortable with. Many pastors as well as lay-members are guilty of not doing things they need to do. I have listed 8 things that you must apply pressure to until you gain control over them. After listing them I will comment on each one to help you work through the process.

Remove Your Self From:

1. Negative thinking
2. Low self-esteem
3. Intimidation
4. Insecurity
5. Drawback reactions
6. Stuck-up reactions
7. Out of control reactions
8. Remaining naïve

Negative Thinking:

The devil does not have the ability to possession a Christian as long as they are in fellowship with the Father. On the other hand, he will seek to confuse as many as he can through negative thinking. The devil does have the ability to attach himself to a Christian's emotions if they are negative thinkers and fill them with fear. When they are full of fear, they are bewitched, (Galatians 3:1) which is just as bad as being possessed with an evil spirit.

Please keep in mind: "Death and life are in the power of the tongue: and they that love it shall eat the fruit thereof." (Proverbs 18:21)

You can gain power over negative thinking by changing your speech. Speak life over things that has been revealed as God's desires for your life.

Low Self-esteem:

Low self-esteem is a by-product of not coming to grips with yourself in order to stay focused on who you are and what Christ can do through you. When the Lord gives you an assignment, don't wrestle with whether or not you are worthy like Gideon did in the book of Judges. When the angel corrected him, his self-esteem was restored. He rose up and was used by God to bring deliverance to Israel. Keep in mind he is no better than you are. If God gave you an assignment, He has made provisions for you. You are an instrument in His hand.

Intimidation:

Don't be afraid of being called a fool for stretching out on faith. You should not be afraid to take a stand for something when the majority thinks you are crazy. Never allow yourself to be held captive because you are worried about what others think. That is the reason why many folks will not reach their goals in life.

The angel reassured Gideon that it was God's will for him to fight the enemy. He was told not to fear them because the Lord was with him and that he was a mighty man of valor. You must realize that God views you differently from what the enemy will try to make you think.

An alarming number of pastors are easily intimidated because they are afraid of being rejected. You must step-up to the plate and begin making your own tracks in life's trail way because you are not a "pathfinder" but a "trailblazer." Stop watching others make history. You are a "history maker." Mary the mother of Jesus had to come in agreement with the angel in order that the words that he had spoken to her come to pass. There was no one she could patterned herself after, she was the one, the "history maker."

In order to accomplish your goal as a pastor, you will need to resolve it that God is with you. Once God has spoken, take courage and go after the promises.

Insecurity:

David was not an insecure person; on the contrary, he was bold and courageous. When he saw Goliath for the very first time, his instincts did not tell him to run like the others soldiers. David perceived that Goliath needed to be removed.

"And David left his carriage in the hand of the keeper of the carriage, and ran into the army, and came and saluted his brethren. And as he talked with them, behold, there came a champion, the Philistine of Gath, Goliath by name, out of the armies of the Philistines, and spake according to the same words: and David heard them. And all the men of Israel, when they saw the man, fled from him, and were sore afraid. And the men of Israel said, Have ye seen this man that is come up? Surely to defy Israel is he come up: and it shall be, that the man who killeth him, the king will enrich him with great riches, and will give him his daughter, and make his father's house free in Israel. And David spake to the men that stood by him, saying, What shall be done to the man that killeth this Philistine, and taketh away the reproach from Israel? For who is this uncircumcised Philistine, that he should defy the armies of the living God? And the people answered him after this manner, saying, So shall it be done to the man that killeth him. And Eliab his eldest brother heard when he spake unto the men; and Eliab's anger was kindled against David, and he said, Why camest thou down hither? And with whom hast thou left those few sheep in the wilderness? I know thy pride, and the naughtiness of thine heart; for thou art come down that thou mightest see the battle. (1 Samuel 17:22-28)

Eliab was insecure. That's why he attacked David. Being a trained soldier in Saul's army , he should have been an example for David and the rest of his brothers. Eliab lacked the knowledge that David had. That's why he was an inexperienced solider when it came to fighting against Goliath. It is also why he was rejected as king when Samuel came to Jesse's house.

To sum it up, insecurity is a lack of faith in God. When a person doesn't believe, they are giving in to the enemy. Doubt is taking sides against God.

Drawback Reactions:

To introduce you to my next topic I have chosen the following verses:

"Now the just shall live by faith: but if any man draw back my soul shall have no pleasure in him. But we are not of them who draw back unto perdition; but of them that believe to the saving of the soul." (Hebrews 10:38-39)

A just person is a person full of faith, but often misunderstood. They are mistaken as the "big head" that knows everything. They do know what the person who draws back doesn't know. Primarily, they know that God is a rewarder of those who diligently seek him (Hebrews 11:6). Secondly, they know that God is the majority so when they are outnumbered, they know that they don't need a lot of people in their corner to win.

There were many courageous individuals in the bible who obtained a good report because of their faith. When they were faced with oppositions they spoke positive words out of their mouths. They were not afraid of the unknown because their faith was anchored in the Lord.

Once you have received God's command , go on and do what He is requiring of you. Resist the devil because he will tell you that you are not qualified. I agree that it is a dangerous a thing to move without hearing from God, but once you have heard from Him, **Move!**

Stuck-up Reactions:

There are those who need deliverance from being a stuck-up person. Every time God sends someone their way, they put up a wall of resistance, and they will not allow anyone to get through to them because they are stubborn. They actually think that they are never wrong.

Others are stuck-up by being filled with pride. They know within themselves that they need help, but they will not admit it. For the most part, they stay in their comfort zone and are very defensive when they are challenged.

Out-of-control Reactions:

We all need to practice self-control in all areas of our lives, especially when it comes to emotions such as being short-tempered and short-patienced. Without self-control we will not demonstrate the love of God when we are under pressure. The world needs to see stable people. We use the term "rooted and grounded."

As you minister to this generation that is out of control, please remain open minded and sensitive to their needs. If you are not open minded, you will miss the opportunity to minister to them because you will become busy finding faults. God also wants you to be patient as you as deal with people because they need help. Jesus was able to help the woman at the well (John 4:1-42) because he was open-minded. He knew that the woman was living in sin but he did not attack her. Jesus, being filled with compassion, knew exactly how to hold a decent conversation with her without driving her away. Through wisdom he took advantage of the opportunity to set her life in order. She went and spread the news about

Jesus all over the town of Samaria. Many lives were blessed because God used the woman as a witness to win others.

Remaining Naïve:

Most pastors have a zeal for ministry, but they can have it without understanding. If you are not aware of your purpose and are ignorant of the mindset of the people you are dealing with, you are spinning your wheels. If that is the case, all of your energy and excitement are in vain. Let me give you an example.

If you are a person who always walks around saying, "I didn't know that" and others always respond, "Where have you been?", it is saying that you stay in the dark too much. On the first anniversary of September 11th there were ceremonies all over the Nation's capital commemorating the many lives that were lost and every one was wearing some type of pin or button. (Keep in mind that was the talk of the day.) Later that evening, I was line behind a woman in the grocery store who wrote a check for her grocery bill and she asked what the date was? The cashier seemed highly upset with her because she felt that being one year to the date (September 11, 2002) for the victims of the planes that crashed into, The Pentagon, World Trade Center, and Pittsburgh, everybody should know what the date was. The person that wrote the check probably did not see it as a big deal. That form of being naïve of the date was inexcusable to the cashier. Its just like someone saying I did not know that Thanksgiving falls on the fourth Thursday of November every year. Although these two examples might seem excusable for some, it is not that way with everyone else. I find it inexcusable for those who are still showing up at the post office on a federal holiday attempting to buy a money order or to mail an important letter at the counter. My attitude is "get with it." What I am trying to say is, that there are things that society expects you to know and they find it inexcusable when you don't.

If you come across as always being naïve to things that you should know, it reflects upon your intelligence. Some Christians don't know as much as they should because they will not allow themselves to become exposed to anything outside of their religious circle.

Subscribing to the daily newspaper and scanning it to find out what going on around you is one way you can educate yourself. In addition, it is helpful to read community news and other related journals or gazettes that provide information about your community and neighboring counties. I also recommend that you subscribe to the Charisma, Ministry Today and Leadership magazines. These Christian magazines, along with others, will keep you informed as to what's happening in the Body of Christ. You may not agree with every thing that is printed in these magazines but it will help keep you up-to-date.

Word of Advice:

It is not good to attack every article that you read about when you stand in the pulpit to minister. If you do, it will open you up to becoming closed-minded and self-righteous.

When you are fearful, you will always come up with the wrong interpretation.

As we precede further into this chapter I want deal with fear because every reaction that I have discussed up until this point is the result of fear. It is important to understand that faith is the opposite of fear and you can't continue to rely upon your ability to fix anything when you are fearful.

Listed below you will find statements coming from those who only appeared to be strong. They appeared strong on the outside but on the inside they were full of fear. That explains why they drew the wrong conclusions.

"Look, the king of Israel has hired the Hittite and Egyptian kings to attack us!" So they got up and fled in the dusk and abandoned their tents and their horses and donkeys. They left the camp as it was and ran for their lives."
(2Kings 7:6b-7)

The enemy was strong because it was an organized and aggressive people. At this point, they never had an experience where God caused anything to happen to them as He did in the story. They trusted in what they could do. When God caused them to hear a noise, they lost all hope in what they could do, and ran for their lives. They were empty on the inside. When God pulled the covers off their hearts, it showed that they were fearful. When God set His hand against your enemy, they are no competition for you.

"The king got up in the night and said to his officers, "I will tell you what the Arameans have done to us. They know we are starving; so they have left the camp to hide in the countryside, thinking, 'They will surely come out, and then we will take them alive and get into the city.'"
(2Kings 7:12)

Although the prophet had spoken the day before that food would be in the city, the king did not expect it to happen because he was fearful. Like most people, instead of enjoying the blessing of the Lord, he feared the worst.

When you are faithful, you will always speak faith-filled words.

Listed below, you will find that David, Elisha and Jesus were men of power because they knew how to frame their words.

> *"David asked the men standing near him, "What will be done for man who kills this Philistine and removes this disgrace from Israel? Who is this uncircumcised Philistine that he should defy the armies of the living God?"*
> *(1 Samuel 17:26)*

David knew that Goliath had to be removed because he had defied God. He was only concerned about one thing: How much reward is involved? David knew he could do the job because he knew that battle did not belong to him, but it belonged to God.

> *"Don't be afraid," the prophet answered.*
> *"Those who are with us are more than those who are with them." (2 Kings 6:16)*

Because Elisha was a man of faith and power, he allowed nothing to intimidate him. He was never moved by what he saw. He was only moved by what he believed. All through his life, he spoke faith filled words at all times.

> *"When he heard this, Jesus said, "This sickness will not end in death. No, it is for God's glory so that God's Son may be glorified through it." (John 11:4)*

Nothing took Jesus by surprise. Lazarus' sickness was predestined. He purposely stayed where he was for two more days after hearing the news about Lazarus. When he eventually returned to the town of Mary and Martha, it was a perfect opportunity for a miracle.

Everybody thought Jesus had arrived too late to do anything for Lazarus. I agree he arrived too late to heal another sick person but not too late to raise an unquestionably dead man. The greater the problem, the greater the miracle. The resurrection of Lazarus brought in a landslide of souls. (John 11:45)

Those who would not allow their fears to keep them from reaching their destiny:

As you read the following verses you see the following individuals had something in common. They resisted what their flesh did not want to do in order to enjoy the victory.

Jacob:

"And Jacob was left alone; and there wrestled a man with him until the breaking of the day. And when he saw that he prevailed not against him, he touched the hollow of his thigh; and the hollow of Jacob's thigh was out of joint, as he wrestled with him. And he said, Let me go, for the day breaketh. And he said, I will not let thee go except thou bless me. And he said unto him, What is thy name? And he said, Jacob. And he said, Thy name shall be called no more Jacob, but Israel: for as a prince has thou power with God and with men, and hast prevailed." (Genesis 32:24-28)

Jacob's first reaction was to fear, but he resisted it because he knew that in order for him to enjoy total freedom he must return home.

The Afflicted Woman:

"And a certain woman, which had an issue of blood twelve years, and had suffered many things of many physicians, and had spent all that she had, and was nothing bettered, but rather grew worse, when she had heard of Jesus, came in the press behind, and touched his garment. For she said, If I may touch but his clothes, I shall be whole. And straightway the fountain of her blood was dried up; and she felt in her body that she was healed of that plague." (Mark 5:25:28)

The afflicted woman went against the character of the women of her day to receive a miracle for her body.

The Lost Son:

"And when he came to himself, he said, How many hired servants of my father's have bread enough and to spare, and I perish with hunger! I will arise and go to my father, and will say unto him, Father, I have sinned against heaven, and before thee, and am no more worthy to be called thy son: make me as one of thy hired servants. And he arose, and came to his father, But when he was yet a great way off, his father saw him, and had compassion, and ran, and fell on his neck, and kissed him." (Luke 15:17-20)

The above individuals had to resist what seemed hard in order to enjoy their victory.

As I prepare to wrap up this chapter I would like to recap a few stories I discussed. Jacob was afraid of Esau because of their past relationship, but he overcame his fears and returned to the land of blessings.

David was told he was not able to defeat Goliath, but he would not allow the king to cause him to become fearful to fight.

The enemy of the children of Israel and the four leprous men were afraid to face what they heard, therefore they lost all their possessions in the wilderness.

The king's porter in the story of the four leprous men did not enjoy the blessings of the Lord because of fear and the words of his mouth.

The afflicted woman had to resist whatever the devil tried to tell in order for her to be healed from the issue of blood.

The lost son had to swallow his pride, rise up over his fears and return to his father's house in order to be restored.

I close this chapter by recording the following scripture:

"For God hath not given us the spirit of fear; but of power, and of love, and of a sound mind." (2 Timothy 1:7)

CHAPTER 8

DOUBLE MINDED

—ⵡ—

I believe that being double minded is one of the leading reasons why many pastors are experiencing defeating when it comes to church growth. Most people who are double minded would never admit to it. That's why it is difficult to get them turned around. The number one reason why they will not admit to it is because the scripture states, "a double minded man is unstable in all his ways." Pride will not let a person admit to the fact that he is unstable in <u>all his ways</u>. You may get a person to admit to a few, but not all. I also believe that it is an embedded problem.

I want to pause and remind you of the statement I made in the introduction. This book was not written to attack any one, but to address issues that will assist those seeking help. Please don't leave this book thinking that every pastor who leads a small church is double minded or has the entire list of problems that are listed throughout this book. There are pastors who have the ability to handle the bible well. They can preach much better than some pastors who have large congregations. In spite of their ability to accurately handle the word of God, they are unstable. For that reason they are stagnated.

I was watching a telecast one Sunday evening and I noticed that the pastor who was on the television could not preach that well, but he has a large congregation. I believe his church is growing because he knows how to get things done. Everything he does is with class and style. Regardless to his preaching abilities, he is appealing to his audience and attracting large numbers because he is single minded in the way he leads.

We must endeavor to keep our words and not have a lot of unfinished business. A talker knows more than they actually does. In order to overcome this matter of having unfinished business, one must stick to the task until it is completed. Keep in mind God will bless what you **do,** not what you know or think. A double minded person is also a person that feeds off public success but privately they are unstable.

I would like to take you to the familiar story of Samson. He was a public success but his private life was a mess. He took the anointing for granted. As long as he had his strength when it was time to fight, he was satisfied. Some pastors are the same way. As long as they have a sermon when it is time to preach, they are satisfied. Please know that we are to measure success based upon our ability to finish what we start and not how we perform in the pulpit. Preaching is not a guarantee that you have it altogether. Below I have listed Samson's public successes.

"And the woman bare a son, and called his name Samson: and the child grew, and the Lord blessed him. And the Spirit of the Lord began to move him at times in the camp of Dan between Zorah and Eshtaol." (Judges 13:24-25)

"Then went Samson down, and his father and his mother, to Timnath, and came to the vineyards of Timnath: and, behold, a young lion roared against him. And the Spirit of the Lord came mightily upon him, and he rent him as he

would have rent a kid, and he had nothing in his hand: but he told not his father or his mother what he had done."
(Judges 14:5-6)

"And when he came unto Lehi, the Philistines shouted against him: and the Spirit of the Lord came mightily upon him, and the cords that were upon his arms became as flax that was burnt with fire, and his bands loosed from off his hands. And he found a new jawbone of an ass and put forth his hand, and took it, and slew a thousand men therewith."
(Judges 15:14-15)

In spite of Samson's public success, he was unstable. He was double minded and this caused him to float from one relationship to another. The Spirit of God eventually departed from him because he did not reverence God's gift. It was only after he was turned over to the enemy that he turned to God in repentance.

The Solution:

In order to get free you must not live in denial. If you know that you are guilty of any of the following, you need to correct it.

1. Procrastination
2. Always changing your mind
3. Never completing what you start
4. Cannot keep your word
5. Unpredictable
6. Always late and forgetful

The Plan

"But seek ye first the kingdom of God, and his righteous-
ness; and all these things shall be added unto you."
(Matthew 6:33)

I believe that this scripture is the greatest of all when it comes to organizing one's life and establishing a single mind. God is the strength of your life. If your life is out of order and God is not first, everything is going to be chaotic.

We have been called to stay close to the Father. He protects our mind from many forms of distraction; The enemy will seek to crowd your life with things that really don't matter.

"Draw nigh to God, and he will draw nigh to you.
Cleanse your hands, ye sinners; and purify your hearts,
ye double-minded. Be afflicted, and mourn, and weep:
let your laughter be turned to mourning, and your joy to
heaviness. Humble yourselves in the sight of the Lord,
and he shall lift you up." (James 4:8-10)

Martha, the sister of Mary, could not figure out why her sister wouldn't voluntarily come and help her work in the kitchen. Mary was more concerned about the most important part. She chose to sit at the feet of Jesus and hear the word. Martha on the other hand chose to concern her self with a form of busyness that kept her mind confused. I have come to realize that devil seeks to confuse those that he can't lead out of the church.

You can train your mind by speaking to yourself and commanding the enemy to release those things that he seeks to use against you. Once you defeat him, you must come up with a plan of action and document everything you do so you can stay on task. A legitimate plan is more than thoughts.

That's why I stress that you must write it down and do it. You will eventually gain enough victory in this area until you will not need to write down everything for the rest of your life. It is for the sake of training your self until you get in shape.

CHAPTER 9

PRAYERLESSNESS

It has reached the point where a pastor must make prayer a priority if he plans to grow. Many groups are forced to close down because people are either dying off, or they are just walking away. Most small churches are experiencing no new growth whatsoever. You must ask God to show you what's wrong. He will reveal to you why your church is not growing. Once the truth is revealed, don't live in denial. If you fail to face reality, you will watch others grow while you continue to decrease.

Prayer is the key to everything we will embark upon whether we pray individually or corporately. Throughout the bible we have the examples of those who obtained a good report. It was a result of them being faithful to the promise and demonstrating the power of prayer. On the other hand, we read about those who fell into temptation because they did not have a prayer life and they did not walk by faith. Jesus described it best in the Garden of Gethsemane when he found his disciples sleeping.

"And he cometh unto the disciples, and findeth them asleep, and saith unto Peter, What, could ye not watch with me one hour? Watch and pray, that ye enter into temptation: the

*spirit indeed is willing, but the flesh is weak."
(Matthew 26:40-41)*

For those that feel like giving up because their churches are not growing, think on these words:

"AND He spake a parable unto them to this end. that men ought always to pray and not faint [give up]." (Luke 18:1)

If you are a victim of having a poor prayer life, you are suffering from something other than just being lazy, untrained, or too busy to pray. The problem is deeper than what is on the surface. It is going to take more than reading a book or attending a Prayer Conference. Prayerlessness is a by-product of one or more of the following emotions.

Sorrow
Frustrations
Fears
Depression
Worrying

"And when he rose up from prayer, and was come to his disciples, he found them sleeping for sorrow." (Luke 22:45)

If you are a person who worries excessively about things, it is a sign that you are trying to fix them through mind powers. Worrying will not add to your stature. You need to stop playing God and release your worries to Him, because nothing will get done until you do.

Prayer is talking to God. Many pastors pray 2 minutes or less per session. That is saying that they can't be saying too much to God. Therefore, "they have not because they ask not" (James 4:2). Faith is speaking those things that are not as though they are. The revelation to this is, if a person is not saying anything, they don't have faith for that area of concern. Any thing that you are overly concern about is actually what you are worrying about.

Another problem I find is that most pastors are procrastinators when it comes to taking care of personal responsibilities. I know they want to put the church ahead of their family, but it only places stress upon their household and increases problems. They must balance their priorities. For example, If they are in too much debt, they need to get on the phone and work with the creditors instead of avoiding them. They will be surprised how much better they will feel once they get their business straightened out. Keep in mind, any form of accomplishment will add strength to your prayer life.

These are stressful times and everyone is struggling with the cares of this life. When a Pastor doesn't have the ability to keep up with the demands placed upon him/her, he has a tendency to become very self-conscience. This will lead him to feeling insecure about the things that he is called to do. Stay alert because every worry that God has delivered you from, Satan will try to bring them back into your life at some point.

In the early years of pastoring I was in sorrow because I was suffering from many silent frustrations. It ate up my prayer life and all I wanted to do was sleep when I came home in the evenings. You might ask what I did. Firstly, I began to expose myself to other things of interest such as:

Taking up a hobby with a friend.
I started an exercise program.
I took tennis lessons.

The above list started restoring my mind. As I started feeling good about myself, I began to actually pray stronger prayers because I felt less sorrowful. After all, the scripture teaches that we should come boldly before the throne. If you are feeling sad you can't do that. I have come to realize when I am going through something; it is not good for me to go into isolation. I have learned to mingle with people because God has positive people stationed along the way that will encourage me when I am discouraged. Everybody needs some form of outlet. Lastly, I kept "a things to do list." I want to repeat; it is surprisingly how small accomplishments strengthen your prayer life.

From time to time I come across another form of sorrow among pastors who are bothered because they have a minister or two in their congregation that they feel threatened by. When that is the case, they will worry about one or two things.

About being replaced.
About a minister taking some of the members and starting a new church.

These worries will cause silent sorrow, which will eat away one's prayer life. Instead of staying focused on the vision, that person will become consumed with watching his back because the devil will use this to cause him to fear and worry about things that are far from the truth. Get renewed and get to work on what God has given you. What you can't fix, leave alone. What ever you do, stop trying to control or monitor every one's actions. If you have some disloyal ministers, turn them over to God. If you can't reason with them, it is best that they move on.

Pastors who have time for prayer have worked through a process. They have a story to tell. It will work for you like it did for others as you work through your process.

Once you get freed from various worries that have eaten away at your prayer life, you must delegate assignments to your staff and members. Inform them of the importance of your prayer life and of the studying of God's word. Satan is cunning; periodically he will seek to get you tied up into minor task that others should be doing. If you do, it will take you back to being stressful all over again. Remember stress leads to sorrow and sorrow leads to sleep.

Peter refused to allow Satan to take him back to the poor prayer life that he had when he was in the garden with Jesus. That is why in the follow passage he and his fellow apostles came up with a solution.

"AND in those days, when the number of the disciples was multiplied, there arose a murmuring of the Grecians [Grecian Jews] against the Hebrews, because their widows were neglected in the daily ministration. Then the twelve call the multitude of the disciples unto them, and said, It is not reason that we should leave the word of God, and serve tables. Wherefore, brethren, look ye out among you seven men of honest report, full of the Holy Ghost [Spirit] and wisdom, whom we may appoint over this business. But we will give ourselves continually to prayer, and to the ministry of the word." (Acts 6:1-4)

The Disciples Before Pentecost:

When you read about Jesus and his three disciples in the garden, the disciples were sorrowing over the conversation that Jesus had with them in John chapters 14-16. Before this point, Jesus had periodically said to them that "the Son of man shall be betrayed into the hands of men: And they shall kill him, and the third day he shall be raised again." It never sank in before, but this time it did. After the Last Supper Jesus took Peter, James and John with him into the garden of Gethsemane to pray. They could not stay awake because they were worried. The following verse sums it all up and reveals the fact that their worries had turned into sorrow.

"Then said some of his disciples among themselves, What is this that he saith unto us, A little while, and ye shall not see me: and again, a little while, and ye shall see me: and, again, a little while, and ye shall see me: and, Because I go to the Father? They said therefore, What is this that he saith, A little while? we cannot tell what he saith. Now Jesus knew what they were desirous to ask him, and said unto them, Do ye inquire among yourselves of that I said, A little while, and ye shall not see me: and again, a little while, and ye shall see me? Verily, verily, I say unto you, That ye shall weep and lament, but the world shall rejoice: and ye shall be sorrowful, but your sorrow shall be turned into joy." (John 16:17-20)

The disciples meant well as they followed Jesus, but they lacked the power of the Holy Spirit, which explains their prayerlessness. For that reason, they did not have the compassion that Jesus had until after they were filled. They tried to please God based upon their human ability. After Jesus was taken up in heaven, they learned that prayer was the key to their success.

"And it came to pass, when the time was come that he should be received up, he steadfastly set his face to go to Jerusalem, And sent messengers before his face: and they went, and entered into a village of the Samaritans, to make ready for him. And they did not receive him, because his face was as though he would go Jerusalem. And when his disciples James and John saw this, they said, Lord, wilt thou that we command fire to come down from heaven, and consume them, even as Elias did? But he turned, and

rebuked them, and said, Ye know not what manner
of spirit ye are of." (Luke 9:51-55)

"And, behold, one of them which were with Jesus
stretched out his hand, and drew his sword, and struck
off his ear. Then said Jesus unto him, Put up again thy
sword into his place: for all they that take the sword shall
perish with the sword." (Matthew 26:51-52)

The Apostles After Pentecost:

The disciples' problem was not corrected at the rebuke of Jesus in the garden when he kept waking them up and challenging them to keep watch. It was only corrected after Pentecost when they were filled with the Holy Spirit. This corrected the spiritual deficit that was in their lives and their sorrow was turned into joy.

When the disciples were filled on the day of Pentecost, they were no longer referred to as disciples but as apostles who moved into full stream ministry. The accomplishment that they obtained in the first few chapters of the book Acts proves that they had a plan of action. Their commitment to the great commission caused them to quickly overcome those things that had previously eaten away their prayer lives. After Pentecost they were men of prayer and they turned the world upside down.

"NOW Peter and John went up together into the temple at
the hour of prayer, being the ninth hour. And a certain man
lame from his mother's womb was carried, whom they laid
daily at the gate of the temple which is called Beautiful, to
ask alms of them that entered into the temple; Who seeing
Peter and John about to go into the temple asked an alms.
And Peter, fastening his eyes upon him with John, said,
Look on us, And he gave heed unto them, expecting to

receive something of them. Then Peter said, Silver and gold have I none; but such as I have give I thee: In the name of Jesus Christ of Nazareth rise up and walk." (Acts 4:13)

"Now when they saw the boldness of Peter and John, and perceived that they were unlearned and ignorant men, they marveled; and they took knowledge of them, that they had been with Jesus." (Acts 4:13)

"And when they had prayed, the place was shaken where they were assembled together; and they were all filled with the Holy Ghost, and they spake the word of God with boldness." (Acts 4:31)

Praying With Understanding:

There are many prayer groups who meet for prayer on a regular basis. The fact that they are zealous about praying is a good thing, but some of them lack understanding. Any time we do something and lack understanding, it is in vain. Most Christians are familiar with some type of prayer group such as:

1. Noonday prayer warriors
2. Intercessory prayer team
3. Seniors' prayer group
4. Multi church prayer meeting
5. Mid-week prayer meeting
6. Neighborhood prayer team

I have cited three events that took place in the United States. These events are examples of how people can pray without understanding.

Elian Gonzalez Case.

Elian's mother along with others decided that they wanted to come into the United States from Cuba. They illegally attempted to enter this country on a raft or some type of boat. Since she was divorced from her husband, she had custody of Elian. In their trying to reach Miami they ran into some trouble, and every one drowned except the boy. Once he was discovered, the family who was waiting for them, recovered him. Word eventually reached his father who was back in Cuba. When he found out that his son was alive, but his ex-wife was dead, he wanted his son to return to Cuba. The episode turned into a long battle between the families here in the U.S. and the father. Once it was exposed by the media, everyone got involved and began to voice their opinion. The case was eventually turned over to the Supreme Courts to decide what to do. They eventually decided that the father was his legal guardian and his wishes overruled everyone else's. Some prayer groups actually got involved and began to pray that the Lord would touch the father's heart and let his son stay here because they felt he would have a better life here. The case ended with the father coming here to gain custody of his child and returning back to Cuba.

The reason why God did not honor the prayer groups' prayers is because the father is the head of his house and once he made the decision, the case was closed. God instituted that the man be head of his house. It has nothing to do with communism. God is not going to violate His structure for the family to please someone's emotional attachment to a person. We must not under estimate God's ability to take care of the boy no matter what country he lives in.

President Bush Declaring War on Iraq

When the president threatened to go to war against Iraq, many people disagreed and became fearful. Many groups protested in the streets and around the world. Many prayer groups also prayed against the war. The scriptures state that in the last days there will be wars and rumors of wars. This war was an event that is reflecting bible prophecy. For those prayer group that don't know how to interpret Last Days events will waste their time praying against things that God will allow to happen. Every Christian must realize that the president has boundaries. He will never do anything over that which God allows. Presidents will make decisions that are going to seem unfavorable to many Christians before it's over. When these decisions are lined-up with bible prophecy, no matter how evil they may seem, it is going to come to pass. The problem is that many prayer group lacks understanding but yet they are devout in their praying. That explains why we went to war in spite of many prayer warriors.

The Terri Schiavo Case

Like many cases this case got out of hand. Michael and Terri Schiavo discussed that if anything happened to either one of them, they did not want to be kept artificially alive. Not long after the conversation with her husband Terri had a heart attack which left her in a critical state. Her husband tried everything possible to help her. After many experimental tests, it was discovered that they made a mistake and Terri would remain in a vegetative state. Michael decided to sue the hospital. He won his case. He eventually came to the decision that his wife was not getting any better, and he decided to remove the feeding tube which was in keeping with what he and his wife had discussed. Upon him taking actions as the head of his house, he was met with opposition.

The battle continued on for many years and eventually every one was aware of the case. The government got involved. The President and Congress were called upon to intervene. After deliberating, they realized it was better to leave it alone. Michael never professed to be a saint, but he is the head of his house. The case ended with Michael's instruction being carried out. He was permitted to that because he is the head of his house. Please understand God is not going to violate his order just because folks' emotions are running rampant. If the government had ruled against Michael, every man would have been violated because the law backs a man as the head of his house.

As I conclude this chapter, I admonish you to use the authority you have as a prayer warrior and an intercessor. Move into the realm of the supernatural with authority and understanding so you can gain victory over those things that have come to stop your progress.

"Let us therefore come boldly unto the throne of grace, that we may obtain mercy, and find grace to help in the time of need." (Hebrews 4:16)

CHAPTER 10

WEAK

—⚏—

In chapter nine I covered the fact that prayerlessness is one of the reasons why some churches are not growing. You don't have to be a rocket scientist to figure out that if a church is prayer less, it will result in being a weak church. With that being said, it brings you to this chapter. In this chapter you will find seven reasons why we have so much weakness in the body of Christ.

1. Fear

And Caleb stilled the people before Moses, and said," Let us go up at once, and possess it; for we are well able to overcome it". But the men that went up with him said," We be not able to go up against the people; for they are stronger than we." And they brought up an evil report of the land which they had gone to search unto the children of Israel, saying," The land through which we have gone to search it, is a land that eateth up the inhabitants thereof; and all the people that we saw in it are men of great stature. And there we saw the giants, the sons of A-nak ,which come of the giants; and we were in our

sight as grasshoppers , and so we were in their sight."
(Numbers 13:30-33)

In order to get a full understanding of this discussion, I recommend that you read the entire 13th chapter of Numbers. The story teaches that Moses sent out 12 spies, one representing each tribe. When they returned, ten of the spies proved to be fearful because they trusted in the flesh. They could not enjoy the fruit of the land because they were afraid of the enemy. They brought back an evil report after searching the land. The information that they found out about the Promised Land was not information that they needed to share with God so that He could look for another plan. God knew that there were giants in the land before He called Moses to go to Egypt. However, the information was for Moses because it revealed to him who he had working with him. It turned out that only two of the twelve men he sent out were courageous enough to help him accomplish what God had spoken. Although all of the spies brought back the large fruit of the land, ten of them were too afraid to possess the land. They came back declaring that they were no match for the people that dwelled in the land. The inhabitant of the land were only characters that God had raised up so that his power would be seen in the earth. When the Lord got through with the enemy, the rest of the world knew that it was He who was fighting the battle. Enemies will come, but they are not our worries; they are only a problem that has presented itself. This generation is guilty like the children of Israel. Both act like God is so far away up in heaven until He doesn't know what's happening on planet earth. I have a favorite saying that says, **"The greater the problem, the greater the victory."** I also believe that a problem is only an opportunity to see another miracle.

When Caleb saw the giants he was not afraid, because he was focused on the promise. He walked by faith, and said that they were well able to overcome them. Caleb did not forget what God did to Pharaoh and the Egyptians in the land of Egypt or at the Red Sea.

The children of Israel who walked out of Egypt, died in the wilderness. Only Caleb and Joshua lived to enter into the Promised Land. The rest of the people died because of their fear and their refusal to trust God. They would not abandon their old mind set.

I would like to put this event in perspective with today's church. You are on the scene. If you are going to receive what God has for you, you need to abandoned your thinking and become deprogrammed so you won't allow fear to keep you from reaching your destiny. You must become reprogrammed so you will only move by what God says and not by what you see. I admonish you to change your thinking through the renewing of your mind. One way to renew your mind is to read scriptures that records the miracles of Jesus on a regular basis. By meditating upon them you will become miracle minded. Once your mind has been renewed, your courage will rise to a level you have never experienced before. There are pastors who are trying to do the work of the Lord yet they are stressed because of all kinds of problems and setbacks that are in their churches. Many are contemplating giving up the ministry because they are paralyzed with fear and intimidation.

To stand in the office of a pastor is like facing a giant. You must face those things that pose as a threat to you through the power of God. It is His anointing that assists you in accomplishing your goals. Some pastors face their giants like Caleb's while others retreat like the fearful spies we read about. The next time the enemy threaten you, think on these verses:

"No weapon that is formed against thee shall prosper; and every tongue that shall rise against thee in judgment thou shalt condemn. This is the heritage of the servants of the Lord, and their righteousness is of me, saith the Lord."
(Isaiah 54:17)

"What shall we then say to these things? If God be for us, who can be against us?" (Romans 8:31)

"Ye are of God, little children, and have overcome them: because greater is he that is in you, than he that is in the world." (1 John 4:4)

2. Bitterness

"And when they saw him afar off, even before he came near unto them, they conspired against him to slay him. And they said one to another, behold, this dreamer cometh. Come now therefore, and let us slay him, and cast him into some pit, and we will say, Some evil beast hath devoured him: and we shall see what will become of his dreams."
(Genesis 37:18-20)

Joseph's brothers were too bitter to see that the hand of the Lord was upon his life. Their bitterness and anger did not stop his dreams from coming to pass.

If you are harboring any form of unforgiveness in your heart, it will turn into bitterness if you don't let it go. Many pastors are stagnated because of bitterness. It is through a pure heart that we serve others.

"Unto the pure all things are pure: but unto them that are defiled and unbelieving is nothing pure: but even their mind and conscience is defiled." (Titus 1:15)

3. Low Self-esteem

"And he bowed himself, and said, What is thy servant, that thou shouldest look upon such a dead dog as I am?" (II Samuel 9:8)

Mephibosheth was a victim of low self-esteem. The Jews customarily deemed a person with a handicap as a second-class citizen. Other groups that were considered second-class citizens were beggars, lepers and the lame. He also suffered shame and fear because his father, grandfather and uncles all died in battle on the same day. When tragedy took place in the family of that magnitude, it was a sign that God was not pleased with the House of Saul. The good part about the story is Mephibosheth did not have to pay for the sins of his grandfather. Everyone must give an account for himself. After the fall of his family, he felt like many of the old patriarchs we read about in the bible who suffered loss. He explained trouble as the hand of the Lord being against him. That is why Mephibosheth called himself a dead dog. He was a prince, but he was bound by his circumstances. Just as David showed him kindest in the story, God wants to do the same for you.

Low self-esteem is not a permanent condition or problem. It can easily be corrected by letting go of the past, facing what you fear, forgiving yourself, stop feeling sorry for yourself and finding fulfillment in the things that you accomplish.

As I review the creation in the first chapter of Genesis, I note that God created something every day and declared that it was good. That tells me that we should accomplish something every day that we can look upon, and feel a sense of pride in the fact that we have been productive. This accomplishment will greatly impact our confidence, which is our faith. People who are full of faith are not easily discouraged. Last, but not least, people who are not easily discouraged are strong.

The problem with many Christians, including pastors, is that too many days go by without them accomplishing anything. For that reason when they come to church, their confidence level is low. That's why the praise team and preachers are pressured to perform. They spend too much time trying to be cheerleaders. Seasoned saints should not come to church seeking motivation all the time. Motivation and self-esteem should come from you feeling good about what you have accomplished, and not from a sermon alone.

4. Laziness

We often describe laziness as a person who lies around all day and gets nothing done. A person who is lazy could be a person who is busy. The only problem is the things that they are busy with are not anything worthwhile. To sum it up, Jonah was a time waster. He stayed busy, but he had his own agenda. The people that God wanted to save, Jonah rejected them. Please don't choose whom you would like to minister unto. That may be your greatest set back. The people you least expect will help you reach the next level. The following scriptures show that he had his own agenda.

"But Jonah rose up to flee unto Tarshish from the presence of the Lord, and went down into it, to go with them unto Tarshish from the presence of the Lord." (Jonah 1:2)

"And he prayed unto the Lord, and said, I pray thee, O Lord, was not this my saying, which I was yet in my country? Therefore I fled before unto Tarshish: for I knew

that thou art a gracious God, and merciful, slow to anger,
and of great kindness, and repentest thee of the evil.
Therefore now, O Lord, take, I beseech thee, my life from
me: for it is better for me to die than to live." (Jonah 4:2-3)

5. Stubbornness

There is nothing that a person will do that will surprise God. He knew what type of person Cain was going to be before the foundation of the world. In the scripture below you will find that Cain was stubborn. His gift was not accepted because he refused to do it God's way. When he was confronted, he still resisted God. He remained restless throughout his life time. Restless people can not be trusted.

"But unto Cain and to his offering he had not respect.
And Cain was very wroth, and his countenance fell.
And the Lord said unto Cain, Why art thou wroth? And why
is thy countenance fallen? If thou doest well, shall thou
not be accepted? And if thou doest not well, sin lieth at the
door. And unto thee shall be his desire, and thou shalt rule
over him. And Cain talked with Abel his brother: and it
came to pass, when they were in the field, that Cain rose up
against Abel his brother, and slew him. And the Lord said
unto Cain, Where is Abel thy brother? And he said,
I know not: Am I my brother's keeper?

6. Unteachable

In order to be successful, you must be willing to listen to the counsel of those whom God will send your way to instruct you. It is possible for you to be doing things that are not good. Moses was a mighty man, yet he did not know how to divide his work-load. He was doing it alone until his father-in-law came to visit and advised him as to how to better serve the people. It was good thing that he was teachable. We can't always say that about every body. There are things that a pastor may do that are not good. Regardless to how much God uses him/her; there are times when they need the assistance of someone. Either in the business of the church or in the pastoral area. Whichever the case, please don't avoid the counsel because it will cost you dearly if you remain un-teachable.

7. Undisciplined.

"And Rebekah heard when Isaac spake to Esau his son. And Esau went to the field to hunt for venison, and to bring it. And Rebekah spake unto Jacob her son, saying Behold, I heard thy father speak unto Esau thy brother, saying, Bring me venison, and make me savoury meat, that I may eat, and bless thee before the Lord before my death. Now therefore, my son, obey my voice according to that which I command thee. Go now to the flock, and fetch me from thence two good kids of the goats; and I will make them savoury meat for thy father, such as he loveth: And thou shalt bring it to thy father, that he may eat, and that he may bless thee before his death. And Jacob said to Rebekah his mother, Behold, Esau my brother is a hairy man, and I am a smooth man: My father peradventure will feel me, and I shall seem to him as a deceiver, and I shall bring a curse upon me, and not a blessing. And his mother said unto him, Upon me be thy curse, my son: only obey my voice, and go fetch me them." (Genesis 27:5-13)

Rebekah wanted Jacob to be blessed so badly until she disregarded her husband as the head of the household. She took matters into her own hands. Because of her undisciplined ways she actually lost both of her sons. Jacob had to flee for his life and Esau rebelled against her so strongly that there was no relationship between the two of them. Rebekah vanished into history. Her name was not mentioned anymore until it spoke of her grave. It is obvious that she died because of depression.

In order to reap the blessings of God, we must live a disciplined live. The twelve men that followed Jesus left all to follow him. In spite of their mistakes they continued to follow him. They eventually got it together. To be a good disciple we must forsake all and follow him.

The Process:

There is a sequence to being strong, victorious and courageous. If you are struggling with a weakness, I want to encourage you because the opposite of being weak is to be strong. Samson got into trouble because he attached himself to weak things. He became a competitor instead of being in a class all by himself. He competed for recognition and acceptance. He did not need to do that because when the Spirit came upon him no one could defeat him. When it came to comparing his strength against another man's strength, there was no competition. There are many lessons to learn from Samson and one of those lessons is: to watch what comes out of your mouth. The following statement came to pass because he spoke it out of his mouth.

"And it came to pass, when she pressed him daily
with her words, and urged him, so that his soul was vexed
unto death; That he told her all his heart, and said unto her,
That hath not come a razor upon mine head;
for I have been a Nazarite unto God from my mother's
womb: if I be shaven, then my strength will go from me,
and I shall become weak, and be like any other man."
(Judges 16:16-17)

Joseph In His Temptation:

The hardship Joseph faced as young man is to be admired. Having to grow-up with stepbrothers who hated him and to have his father to also misinterpret his dream had to be frustrating. Yet he kept on loving God and made the best out of every situation he found himself in.

When Potiphar wife tried to seduce him, he made an astounding statement concerning his conviction as a man of God.

"There is none greater in this house than I; neither hath he kept back any thing from me but thee, because thou art his wife: how then can I do this great wickedness, and sin against God?" (Genesis 39:9)

Because he took that stand, he found himself in jail. He could have easily given up and turned his back on God. Instead, he got closer to the Lord and was rewarded.

David In His Temptation:

David did not do so well when he was tempted with sexual sins.

"AND it came to pass, after the year was expired, at the time when kings go forth to battle, that David sent Joab, and his servants with him, and all Israel; and they destroyed the children of Ammon, and besieged Rabbah. But David tarried still at Jerusalem. And it came to pass in an eveningtide, that David arose from off his bed, and walked upon the roof of the king's house: and from the roof he saw a woman washing herself; and the woman was very beautiful to look upon. And David sent and inquired

after the woman. And one said, Is not this Bath-sheba,
the daughter of Eliam, the wife of Uriah the Hittite? And
David sent messengers, and took her; and she came in
unto him, and he lay with her; for she was purified from
her uncleanness: and she returned unto her house. And the
woman conceived, and sent and told David, and said,
I am with child." (2 Samuel 11:1-5)

Somewhere, along the way David became burned out
and lost his conviction for what was pure in the sight of God.
He took matters into his own hands and got into trouble. The
devil only needed a space and he took advantage of David.
He did not act like Joseph when tempted. Joseph got away
from temptation quickly, but David lingered around the
balcony until his flesh had gotten the best of him.

"Let no man say when he is tempted, I am tempted of God:
for God cannot be tempted with evil, neither tempteth he
any man: But every man is tempted, when he is drawn
away of his own lust, and enticed. Then when lust hath
conceived, it bringeth forth sin: and sin, when it is
finished, bringeth forth death." (James 1:13-15)

Turning Weakness into Ministry:

Before I bring this chapter to a close, I would like to
encourage you with the fact that God can turn your experience into ministry.

My mother was sickly during our child hood years.
Therefore I grew up fearing the worst. When she got sick,
we got little sleep. We learned not to make noise in the home
because we did not want to disturb her. As a child I spent
many hours reading the bible and praying for God's help.
Although I didn't like to read, the bible brought relief to my
fears. Those days were a part of my training for what I am

doing today. Although fear is viewed as a weakness, it played an important role in my having an in-depth knowledge of the bible. Today I am skillful in the using the bible as my main source of reference as I write, preach and conduct training seminars.

CHAPTER 11

FIGHTING SPIRIT

—〜〜—

We live in a world that offers a variety of styles, cultures and beliefs. When it comes to the church, we have to accommodate this diverse generation, because everyone belongs to God. Keep in mind, I said accommodate, but we must not compromise the righteousness of the gospel. We are experiencing differences in the way we worship, the way we dress, whether or not women are called to preach, the correct formula for baptism and many more. All these areas are disputable issues, and they will not be resolved before Christ returns for his church. It is true every body can't be right. Please know that it is a waste of time to keep fighting each other. God is in charge of the body of Christ. Let Him fix it. He does not want you to go on a crusade fighting other denominations over belief issues. Let's face it, everybody is not going to believe what you believe. If you are guilty, you are fighting something much bigger than your self. Periodically, I come across pastors who are restless because they are consumed with trying to fix the body of Christ. They have lost focus on their purpose of existence as a church. Please keep in mind; everything that you are concerned about, is not up to you to fix. I know I have said that if you can identify a problem, you are part of the solution. However, when it comes to an issue in the body of Christ that is an ongoing feud, God doesn't want you to take it upon your self. In cases like that the best solution is to cover the matter in prayer and leave it alone.

Many who once fought so-called doctrinal issues that were their own hang-ups, have changed. I am aware of a few cases where they came forth and publicly apologized to those whom they spoke against. They came to the revelation that they were wrong. That came about through the power of prayer.

We must come to a level of maturity when we deal with people of diverse backgrounds and practices. I have three examples I would like to share.

Example 1

A relative invited me to speak at his church. When I got there and sat in the pulpit I noticed that I was the only man in the church who had on a necktie. I said to my cousin after ward that he should have said something to me because I have clergy shirts as well as Japanese style shirts that I could have worn. He figured if he told me I would not have accepted. To me that was a small thing. Even if it meant wearing a button-up white shirt, it would not have taken any thing from me, nor would it have effected my anointing. Because of my attitude, the people received me in spite of the fact that I wore a tie.

Example 2

On another occasion I was invited to a church to preach. This place was unattractive and the people could have used some training in church etiquette. I went because I had compassion on them. I ministered without allowing anything to interfere with what was on my heart. A woman testified how she was healed while I was preaching. Although I knew in advance what I was up against, I didn't mind. I went to encourage the people because the pastor had been ill for a long time.

Example 3

I went to another church similar to the previous example. Again I did not allow anything to interfere with what I had gone to do. There was a mother in that church who had been there a long time. She was a faithful member as long as I knew the folks. Some thing happened during the week prior to my going that upset her and she made up her mind that she was never going back to that church. She said for some reason she decided to give it one more try. It was in that service that God spoke to her through what I said that caused her to change her mind. She thanked me for allowing God to use me. She said "I'm going to be alright now".

The three examples were learning experiences for me. I don't allow my personal views to keep me from ministering to people. I go places seeking to help people instead of going to find faults.

As you continue in this chapter, I have provided some advice for how to avoid getting into fights over unimportant matters and win the lost:

1. Don't fight what you don't understand:

Every pastor has something to offer the community as well as the body of Christ. Each should be fully equipped to do the task that he/she is in charge of. That does not mean you know everything. Some of your help may come from another church that is not a part of your denomination. Don't refuse help when it comes from outsiders.

I always apply the following scripture when it I visit a conference or gathering that may differ from my format.

"Wherefore [Ye know this], my beloved brethren,
let every man be swift to hear, slow to speak,
slow to wrath." (James 1:19)

God may be trying to provide your deliverance by introducing you to something that you have not seen done a particular way before. When you draw quick conclusions, you leave no room for God to speak to you.

2. Everything that's different is not wrong:

You may have been praying and asking God to show you what you are doing wrong. He may allow you to come in contact with another ministry that has the missing pieces to your puzzle. The only problem is that they do things differently from what you have deemed as the only way to do it.

If you plan to grow, you must become flexible. By doing so you will gain a wealth of knowledge as to how to implement church growth. The apostle Paul teaches a very powerful lesson on flexibility in the following passages.

"For though I be free from all men, yet have I made myself servant unto all, that I might gain the more. And unto the Jews I became as a Jew, that I may gain the Jews; to them that are under the law, as under the law, that I might gain them that are under the law; To them that are without the law, (being not without law to God, but under the law of Christ,) that I might gain them that are without law. To the weak became I as weak, that I might gain the weak: I am made all things to all men, that I might by all means save

some. And this I do [And I do all things] for the gospel's
sake, that I might be partaker thereof with you."
(1 Corinthians 1:19-22)

Several years ago I was browsing through a Christian magazine. I saw an advertisement for an Evangelistic Outreach Explosion. When I read the information, it sounded very interesting. I decided to go. Before I left, two thoughts were fresh in my mind. (1) Don't fight what you don't understand. (2) Every thing that is different is not wrong. I learned that from an older woman while attending a workshop that dealt with how to start a cell church.

I arrived the day before the event because the first session started early the next morning. I rented a car and checked into my hotel room. I got up early the next morning and had devotion. While I was mediating, the thought revisited me once again "Don't fight what you don't understand. Everything that is different is not wrong." When I got to the place, to my surprise, the sessions were under a tent and everyone was dressed-down. I showed up in a double-breasted suit. I had a mindset of sitting in a pretty church with a bunch of dressed-up folks. When I got under the tent, I was the only one dressed-up. When no one was looking, I took off my tie and later my coat because I wanted to fit in. When we broke for lunch, I found a Wal-mart store and bought some clothes because I did not take any casual clothes other than what I was traveling in. I did that so I could blend in. Although the people were dressed down and did not believe everything I believed, I could not deny the power and the anointing that was under that tent. One thing for sure, I know the presence of God when it is present. I was mature enough to adapt to what was different instead of fighting and resisting it. I had the best time of my life during my stay. When the conference of was over, I also met some new friends. Everyone was blessed because we all had something to share during the conference. It was a healing in disguised.

3. Make an effort to mind your own business:

As you study the life and ministry of Jesus Christ, you will find that he often encountered many religious leaders tempting him. They showed up day after day seeking for reasons to entrap him so that they might find some justification to get rid of him. The following scripture is a good example of someone being a busy body.

> *"AT that time Jesus went on the Sabbath day through the corn; and his disciples were an hungered, and began to pluck the ears of corn, and to eat, **But when the Pharisees saw it**, they said unto him, Behold, thy disciples do that which is not lawful to do upon the Sabbath day."*
> *(Matthew 12:1-2)*

In order for the Pharisees to be able to catch the disciples in the act of picking corn, that meant that they had to skip worshipping in the synagogue to be in the cornfield to find fault with Jesus and his disciples. You would think that highly educated men would have better things to do with themselves than to be snooping in a cornfield. We have that same problem today. Some folks listen to other ministries on the radio or television merely to find fault.

4. Don't live to find faults.

> *"Jesus Went unto the mount of Olives. And early in the morning he came again into the temple, and all the people came unto him; and he sat down, and taught them. And the scribes and Pharisees brought unto him a woman taken in adultery; and when they had set her in the midst, They say*

unto him, Master, this woman was taken in adultery, in the very act. Now Moses in the law commanded us, that such should be stoned: but what sayest thou? This they said, tempting him, that they might have to accuse him. But Jesus stooped down, and with his finger wrote on the ground, as though he heard them not. So when they continued asking him, he lifted up himself, and said unto them, He that is without sin among you, let him first cast a stone at her. And again he stooped down, and wrote on the ground. And they which heard it, being convicted by their own conscience, went out one by one, beginning at the eldest, even unto the last: and Jesus was left alone, and the woman standing in the midst. When Jesus had lifted up himself, and saw none but the woman, he said unto her, Woman, where are those thine accusers? hath no man condemned thee? She said, No man, Lord. And Jesus said unto her, Neither do I condemn thee: go, and sin no more." (John 8:1-10)

Jesus is our perfect example; he defused a situation that could have gotten out of hand. The accusers had a hidden agenda in the first place. They were not interested in the woman's future or her salvation. It was their reputation that they were trying to protect. Jesus' mannerism helped the woman and it also offered help for those that judged the matter.

As I close this chapter I would like to leave a few points:

- Take the beam out of your own eyes first.
- Don't listen to gossip.
- When tempted to comment about another pastor, keep it to yourself.

CHAPTER 12

POOR PREACHING AND TEACHING SKILLS

—m—

As a child, I attended a traditional church with my parents until I became a teenager. I didn't get too much out of that church during those days because the services or the preaching were not geared toward the youth. The church was also lagging behind most of the churches when it came to talented musicians and singers.

Although most churches in the 50's and 60's didn't have youth pastors or youth ministries, they didn't hinder young people who were bold and zealous enough to volunteer to do things in church. Most youth, including myself didn't participate in church. Every now and then you would find one or two who sung or attempted to preach a sermon.

It was not until I joined a newly formed church, organized by my aunt, that I became more active in church. It was at this point that I slowly began to take the initiative about increasing my bible knowledge. I learned as much as I could from that experience, but I was limited because my pastor had an elementary school education.

Later I moved to Savannah, Georgia. From the experience I moved up in my level of knowledge because the pace was a little faster and I was exposed to a little more training.

In 1977, I moved to the Washington, D.C. metro area. In my quest to pursue a church home and maintain my relationship with God, I noticed that I was behind in many ways. My hunger for God began to intensify and that's when I really began to notice that the churches in the south were lagging in preaching and teaching skills. I also noticed that the body of Christ was not where it needed to be in the area of evangelism.

When I look back, I thank God for the early years of experience because it was not a complete waste. Although I missed a lot of training, I was not lagging in the area of integrity and holiness.

It was not until the early eighties that I began to venture outside of my normal circle and realized that I needed to educate my self by studying the bible more carefully. I began to read books by Christian authors, which was a tremendous help in my relating to God. Shortly after that I was introduced to a few nationally known evangelist who had very good preaching and teaching skills. I was excited because I had not experienced that kind of skill up until this point in my life. I attended many of their revivals and seminars when they came to the area. When I was not able to attend their services, I purchased the tapes and studied along with them.

About the same time, I was introduced to a missionary group that held a monthly bible study and I learned how to use the reference and topical bible. All of this happened for me because of my hunger for righteousness.

After I had been gone for a year, I was scheduled to minister at my home church. Upon my return they could see the difference in my preaching.

I said all of that to say that many pastors have poor preaching and teaching skills because they are doing nothing about it. I realize that everybody is not able to attend a college or training center.

However if you are sincere, God will see to it that you get what you need. It actually starts by hungering and thirsting after God's righteousness. Once that takes place, walk through the doors He opens unto you.

"Blessed are they which do hunger and thirst after righteousness: for they shall be filled." (Matthew 5:6)

Listed below are some tips that will help you sharpen your skills in studying the bible:

1. Use a college level dictionary to define words you don't understand.
2. Read other versions of the bible to help you relate to and interpret the scriptures.
3. Read and study the notes in a bible designed for teens because they are loaded with illustrations.
4. Buy a bible dictionary for children with pictures in it.
5. Buy the bible on cassette (Dramatize)
6. Use the Life Application Study Bible
7. View old bible movies.
8. Study and absorb the first five books of the bible.
9. Pay close attention to the first six verses when beginning any chapter because those verses usually sets the pace for the remainder of the chapter.
10. Pay close attention to locations, names, who is speaking, to whom the scripture is speaking , and stop to define any words you don't understand.
11. Pay close attention of the first chapter when studying any book in the bible because the first chapter serves as an outline for the remainder of that book.
12. Highlight scriptures that encourage you the most.

13. Balance your studying with prayer and worship.
14. Free your mind by forgiving and releasing others.
15. Read until you get into the habit of reading more than your routine scriptures.

Some pastors are guilty of creating a small world and they think no one is right but them. God has people in this world that can help you, if you will submit yourself to what's available. I challenge you to venture out of your backyard. You will not agree with everything you hear but eat the fish and throw away the bones.

This generation is starving for the word of God as the scripture says:

> *"Behold, the days come, saith the Lord God, that I will send a famine in the land, not a famine of bread, nor a thirst for water, but of hearing the words of the Lord: And they shall wander from sea to sea, and from the north even to the east, they shall run to and fro to seek the word of the Lord, and shall not find it." (Amos 8:11-12)*

Pray and apply your self to better preaching skills. God will equip you. If you don't, sooner or later your members are going to hear better preaching and may become tempted to leave your church if you do nothing to improve yourself. If you lack preaching skills your congregation is hungry.

CHAPTER 13

LACKS THE ABILITY TO SEPARATE CHURCH DOCTRINE FROM GENERAL PREACHING

—m—

As we look back over the past few years we have been through a variety of major events that have left the world shaken.

1. Sickness
2. Death
3. Murder
4. Unemployment
5. Wars
6. Divorce and separation
7. Severe weather disasters
8. September 11th attack
9. The Anthrax event with the postal service
10. SARS outbreak
11. The Aids epidemic
12. The Tsunami disaster

When people show up at church on Sundays, they have a lot on their minds. Sunday morning is when a church is basically going to attract people. Christians should be on their best behavior and ready to meet the needs of the unchurched. We are fishers of men. We must have good bait if we plan to be successful. They are seeking answers and a peace of mind. They need ministry. Although many of them are guilty of something, they showed up in church because they know that's where they need to be.

The woman that Jesus met at the well in Samaria had a need. Jesus did not attack her. He got her to talk about what was bothering her. The conversation enabled Jesus to win her trust and from that he was able to meet her needs.

> *"And I, if I be lifted up from the earth,*
> *will draw all men unto me." (John 12:32)*

The above verse tells what a preacher should do when he/she stands to minister to a general audience. We should lift up the name of Jesus by preaching the gospel. The gospel is sharing how Jesus was our perfect example. The gospel also reveals the finished work that he completed by dying on the cross for ours sins. The good news is that he paid our sin- debt in full so we can be free. Lifting up the name of Jesus also consists of teaching on repentant and forgiveness of sins so people will understand the importance of receiving and forgiving others.

It is not hard to lead someone to Christ if you teach him or her how to receive salvation. It only seems hard when we attack their problem and don't provide them with solutions. They will listen if you compassionately show them how to become born again and how to live a victorious life.

Any time a minister fails to lift up the name Jesus and fights the audience with his doctrine, he is not operating in the realm of his purpose as a Minister of the gospel. For that reason, it will be in vain. When a minister stands to preach before a general audience that is not the time to drill on his doctrine. You reserve your doctrine for new member's orientation or other related classes. This is done after you have won the person and they want to join your fellowship.

When a person is seeking membership, you introduce them to the following:

1. Who you are (Information about the church)
2. Your vision
3. Your mission statement
4. The church's history
5. The way you worship and why
6. What you believe (Church's doctrine)
7. Contact person

Evangelist style and general preaching should be reserved for the following:

1. Sunday Morning Services
2. Conferences
3. Funerals
4. Family day
5. Holiday services
6. Guest Speaker
7. Revivals
8. Bible study in the workplace

All of the above events serve as a good opportunity to operate as an evangelist. Ninety five percent of your membership possibly came to you through one of the mentioned events.

I have seen bible studies in the work place dissolve because of individuals trying to promote their doctrine in a general bible study. There is a difference between a local church bible study and a general bible study in the work place. I visited a few a bible studies at work over the years. There was one class in particular that was attracting a large group from various denominations. It happened because the person in charge of the class was doing a fantastic job and stayed focus on general teachings. On one occasion while the instructor was teaching, some one asked a question and before long the class went into an uproar. One person became offended and over zealous in defending their doctrinal belief. All of a sudden the class was divided in three groups. (1) Those that believed this person. (2) Those that strongly disagreed. (3) Those that were neutral. The instructor was very skillful and brought the class back to order and continued. Afterward, a friend who thought I should have said something since I was a pastor, approached me. I made her aware of the fact, that it was not my place to take over someone else's class. I also made her aware that the leader of the class handled the matter very well. Pastors must know when to submit to authority and not attempt to usurp authority in every setting.

Another event on the list I previously mentioned is a funeral. This event will possibly attract more people to a small church than any event. Keep in mind it was the funeral that drew the crowd and not the anointing. Since it was the funeral that drew the crowd a pastor should not use it as an opportunity to attack or insult people. Many people have stopped going to church because of remarks pastors have made at funerals.

A funeral is not the time to address the following:

1. Baptism
2. Dress codes
3. Whether or not God called women to preach.
4. Denominations

When a pastor is preparing for a funeral, he should put aside everything he is overly concerned about and use discretion as to how to use this event to share the gospel. Keep in mind everything you are concerned about is not always what is best for you to talk about. There is nothing wrong with being concerned. However, with concern you need to be able to discern matters. When you are discerning, you pray about those things that you don't need to talk about at the moment, and focus on the need. When Jesus ministered in Samaria, he was moved by the need and not the concern. He did not condone the fact that the woman was an adulteress. He knew how to work around the problem and bring salvation to the city.

It is also wise when a pastor is doing a funeral to familiarize him or herself with the program before the funeral service. If you plan to acknowledge family members in your comments, please make sure you acknowledge those that are not members of your congregation as well. I have seen so many families get upset because the pastor only acknowledged those he knew. Maybe you are eulogizing a mother and maybe the mother has other children listed in the obituary that you don't know. That's why I suggested that you get the program in advance so you can rehearse who you need to address. Don't get so carried away with your sermon that you are insensitive as to who is in the audience.

I would like to share four experiences that I noticed while attending a few funerals. In each case the minister missed the opportunity to share the gospel of Jesus Christ.

Hell fire and Brimstone Sermon

I was about 18 years old when an older woman passed away. It turned into a double funeral because one of her nephews who was planning to attend her funeral, died of a massive heart attack as he was preparing to drive to Georgia for her funeral. He lived in the north. Since his death happened close to his aunt's death, the family decided to have a double funeral. This man had ten sisters. His death also brought people who would not have attended the funeral if it were only for the woman. Those who presided over the service were not familiar with the additional crowd . My cousin and I sat up front because she was asked to read the acknowledgements. The church was packed and a large crowd was standing on the outside. One of the pastors, who were an Overseer of the church where the woman belonged, had comments. This Overseer did not know most of the family and was insensitive to the grieving audience. The comments came across sharp and hard-hitting. The remarks sounded like the man went to hell and the woman went to heaven. One of the sisters of the deceased jumped up screaming "that's my brother." She was headed for the pulpit. It took several men to hold her down. The pastor stopped talking and waited until they got the woman calmed down. Afterward the person continued commenting in a negative fashion about those who were unbelievers. They were sentenced to hell no doubt about it. I was very nervous because the people were highly insulted. The anger level was high in that place. My cousin and I couldn't wait to get out of there. We skipped going to the burial site or the reception dinner afterward.

Those who ministered on that day missed an opportunity to share the gospel to the grief stricken audience who needed to be encouraged. With the right approach that could have been a healing experience for those torn by the young man's untimely death.

When you are preparing to minister at funerals, think on these words:

"Behold, I send you forth as sheep in the midst of wolves: be ye therefore wise as serpents, and harmless as doves."
(Matthews 10:16)

"The fruit of the righteous is a tree of life; and he that winneth souls is wise." (Proverbs 11:30)

Nobody is Right, But Us Sermon

My next experience was a funeral where the preacher attacked everybody that did not meet his dress code. From that, he attacked women preachers and the water baptism and etc. Those are disputable issues. A funeral should not serve as an opportunity for a preacher to take pot shots at those that are at his mercy because they have come to pay their final respect to the dead. I personally feel if a funeral draws more to our churches than the anointing, we should cautiously watch our behavior when we stand over God's people. Keep in mind it was the anointing on Jesus' life that drew large crowds. If we cannot draw larger crowds other than at a funeral, it is an indictment against the church.

Defense of Water Baptism Sermon

As I stated in the discussion prior to this one, a funeral is not the place to address your doctrine. Water baptism has nothing to do with a funeral. That tells me that a person who does this is overly concerned with a debate that will be here when the rapture takes place. We cannot make every one believe what we believe. I am not against water baptism because it is a part of the plan of salvation. I have my doctrinal belief but I know when and where to share it. I said this because I assisted at another funeral where this happened. The church was filled with dignitaries and people that did not baptize the way the preacher who spoke did. He really made himself look bad in the service. There was also a large number of youth that could have been targeted but they were not as important as his doctrinal belief. I am concerned about the fact that the harvest is plenteous.

Christians Are No Better Than Sinners Sermon

I was asked to preside over a funeral because the person on the program was not present. The family wanted to start on time, so I began the service. The person did not make the funeral at all, so I continued on. When it was time to turn it over to the eulogists, I was surprised to find that he was overly cautious about the unbelievers. He did not know how to rightly divide the word of God. He made it seem as if becoming a Christian is no better than being a sinner. He was trying to relate to the unchurched, but he made Christians look bad in his delivery. We are not better than them when it comes to receiving salvation. However, if someone accepts Christ in his heart and they die, they will go to heaven. From that perspective he is better than a sinner who will reject the gospel and goes to hell. The unchurched do need to beware that they need to be born again. They are not to become comfortable thinking that Christians are still as filthy rags. The truth of the matter is, when a person is born again, he is a new creature. The old is gone and the new has come. The filthy rags that Jeremiah referred to was when Israel was in a backslidden condition and they were trying to justify their rebellious ways. They deemed unrighteousness as righteousness. Once we are born again, we are no longer filthy rags.

"For he hath made him to be sin for us, who knew no sin;
that we might be made the righteousness of God in him."
(2 Corinthians 5:21)

CHAPTER 14

THE HEAD OF THE CHURCH IN THE WRONG CALLING

—⁂—

*"And he gave some, **apostles; and some, prophets;**
and some, evangelists; and some, pastors and teachers;
for the perfecting of the saints, for the work of the ministry.
For the edifying of the body of Christ: Till we all come in
the unity of the faith, and of the knowledge of the Son of
God, unto a perfect man, unto the measure of the stature
of the fullness of Christ." (Ephesians 4:11-13)*

It is at the discretion of a senior pastor to assign ministers to various positions in the local church. I believe if a minister remains faithful with the assignment, God will reveal to him/her what area of ministry they are called to operate under. Make sure you don't invade into an office that God did not call you into, because everyone has not been called to first level ministry but to second level wherein they are to operate in the ministry of helps. The ministry of helps is just as needful because front line ministers such as pastors need ministers to support them.

There is a vast difference between someone who walks in the office of a Teacher than that of a Sunday school teacher. There is also a vast difference between the office of a Prophet and person who occasionally give a prophecy from the pews. The gifts in Ephesians chapter four are ministry gifts. The person that operates in the five-fold ministry is first and far most a minister of the gospel, with a specialty in a particulate office.

Every female minister is not an Evangelist because that gift is without gender. An Evangelist or Missionary can be a male or female who has the ability to go into dangerous, un-churched areas that are heavily infested with sin and start a revival, which affect the territory both spiritually and economically. They have the ability and authority to establish churches and operate as a pastor until a suitable pastor is appointed to carry on the new work.

It is possible for ministers not to realize that they are in the wrong office, especially if they strongly want to do what they want to do. Some get into the wrong office because others encouraged them to pursue the office and because they felt that was what God wanted them to do. For example an Evangelist could be trying to function as an Apostle. A Teacher could be trying to function as a Pastor or vice –a –versa.

The above paragraph reveals that it is possible for well wishers such as pastors, bishops, family and friends to cause individuals to get off in the wrong office because they have an opinion. People mean well, but they often move by feelings, which causes people to invade into the wrong calling.

I met a teacher who was pastoring but he discovered that he was not a pastor. He had already attempted to pastor two churches before he came into the knowledge that he was in the wrong office. He sought God earnestly because something was not right to him and he was determine not to live in denial any longer. He said it was like trying to take a shower with his socks on. After much prayer and fasting, God revealed to him what office he was supposed to be operating in. He was actually shocked to learn that he was not called to the office of a pastor at all. He humbled himself and stepped down. God told him that he was to teach the word because he was called to the office of a teacher. God instructed him to turn the church over to his son. After he submitted himself to God, he and his son's ministry transformed in a major move of God. Today they are both known worldwide.

I also met a husband and wife team that started a church. The husband assumed that he was to be the senior pastor with his wife as the assistant pastor. They struggled to get the church off the ground but something was not right. One day God revealed to the wife what was wrong. He informed her that she was supposed to be the senior pastor. Her husband was working a full-time job and she was afraid to call him because she was not sure how he was going to respond to what God had said to her. She eventually called him later that day and when she told him what God had said to her, he confirmed that God had spoken to him too. They made the necessary changes and the church took off like water rushing down a hill.

I would like to share one final example of two other pastors who should be operating in the office of an evangelist. They are determined to pastor the church that they are over because they both love the idea of being in charge of people. Because they are in the wrong office, they are always going through unnecessary changes. They can never keep a solid group of people in order to get themselves established. One of them got off on the wrong foot from the start. He went to a church to do a revival and some of the members of the church came to him secretly to complain about the church and the pastor. When the revival was over, he secretly met with those people and started a church. The appropriate thing that he should have done was to go to that pastor and offer his assistance in resolving the problem in the church. If the pastor agreed, he should have supported the pastor until the church got in order and then moved on. He would have been a blessing to the pastor by doing that because the pastor trusted him to come into his church in the first place. He did not prosper because he invaded an office that he was not called into. He betrayed his fellow brother. He reaped what he sowed. The majority of the people eventually left him and went on to another church.

Although he is a good preacher and people responded well to him during the revival, he acted out of order when the revival was over. The anointing that is upon his life is stifled because of manipulation and other games that he often play on people. People are carried away with his abilities, but like Samson he will eventually find himself without power. He has been repeating the same process for nearly twenty years. With the amount of people dying each day he will never impact this generation unless he humble himself and get in his rightful place.

There are an alarming number of ministers in the wrong calling because they don't want to submit to authority. The danger about this is that many of them are coming to the realization that they are not pastors and are unwilling to step down. They have exalted them selves. They are living in denial. Please note the following scriptures:

"Not everyone that saith unto me, Lord, Lord, shall enter into the kingdom of heaven; but he that doeth the will of my Father which is in heaven. Many will say to me in that day Lord, Lord, have we not prophesied in thy name? And in thy name have cast out devils? And in thy name have done many wonderful works? And then I will profess unto them, I never knew you: depart from me, ye that work iniquity." (Matthew 7:21-23)

"For it is written, as I live, saith the Lord, every knee shall bow to me, and every tongue shall confess to God. So then every one of us shall give account of himself to God." (Romans 14:11-12)

There will be those who sincerely work in the wrong office without knowing it and they will die doing so. They will not be judged for not knowing. Their ignorance will be burned, but they themselves will be saved as stated in the following scriptures.

Every man's work shall be made manifest:
for the day shall declare it, because it shall be revealed by
fire; and the fire shall try every man's work of what sort it
is. If any man's work abide which he hath built thereupon,
he shall receive a reward. If any man's work shall be
burned, he shall suffer loss; but he himself shall be saved,
yet so as by fire." (1 Corinthians 3:13-15)

CHAPTER 15

PASTORING FOR THE WRONG REASONS

—∿—

In this chapter you will learn that you should not strive to become a large church for the wrong reasons such as, to impress people, to make a name for your self, or to compete with others, but to simply obey the great commission.

"And Jesus came and spake unto them, saying,
All power is given unto me in heaven and in earth. Go
ye therefore, and teach all nations, baptizing them in the
name of the Father, and of the Son, and of the Holy Ghost:
teaching them to observe all things whatsoever I have
commanded you: and, lo, I am with you always, even unto
the end of the world. Amen." (Matthew 28:18-20)

Please note that God did not call one church to take the city, but <u>together</u> we can!

I have also noticed that many small churches are comfortable being a small (family) church. Some believe that in a large church, a person won't get that personal attention and the pastor does not know everybody. Moses didn't know everybody either because his mission was to deliver the nation of Israel and not only Miriam, Aaron, his nieces and nephews. God never intended for us to know everybody. We must broaden our view. When I lived in the south I had a southern view of Christianity. When I started traveling and visiting large events such national and international conference I began to think worldwide. If you have never been out of this country, it is possible that you read the bible with a United States' mentality. A United States' mentality thinks when the bible states from the east to the west it is only talking about from New York (east) to California (west). Since I travel outside of this country, when I read the bible and when it states from the east to the west. I see the east as Africa, Iran, Asia, Russia, China, India, etc. and I see the west as North America, South America and Canada.

The bigger picture reveals that millions of people are dying without salvation. Please don't limit yourselves only to your own family, race or native culture because we are responsible to preach the gospel to **every creature.** (Mark 16:15)

As you ponder the following scriptures may you sense the urgency to move out of the box of limitation because there is a big world waiting to be evangelized.

*"And there followed him **great multitudes** of people from Galilee, and from Decapolis, and from Jerusalem, and from Judea, and from beyond Jordan." (Matthew 4:25)*

*"WHEN HE was come down from the mountain, **great multitudes** followed him." (Matthew 8:1)*

*"But when he saw the **multitudes,** he was moved with compassion on them, because they fainted, and were scattered abroad, as sheep having no shepherd. Then saith he unto his disciples, the harvest truly is **plenteous**, but the labourers are few." (Matthew 9:36-37)*

*"But when Jesus knew it, he withdrew himself from thence: and **great multitudes** followed him, and he healed them all." (Matthew 12:15)*

*"And **great multitudes** followed him; and he healed them there." (Matthew 19:2)*

*"And as they departed from Jericho, a **great multitude** followed him." (Matthew 20:29)*

*"Then **many** of the Jews which came to Mary, and had seen the things which Jesus did, believed on him." (John 11:45)*

*"Then they that gladly received his word were baptized: and the same day there were added unto them about **three thousand** souls." (Acts 2:41)*

*"And they, continuing daily with one accord in the temple, and breaking bread from house to house, did eat their meat with gladness and singleness of heart. Praising God, and having favour with all people. And the Lord **added to the church daily** such as should be saved." (Acts 2:46-47)*

Make no mistakes about it, God does all things well and He calls us according to His purpose. Pastoring is about serving God's people and fulfilling His will on earth and not our own. It is a dangerous thing for individual to enter into pastoral ministry for money or for some personal reason. When a person operates as a pastor for the wrong reasons, they usually end on a sad note or they will struggle for the rest of their lives. They will frustrate the gift and will also abuse the faithful people who support them. The reason I call it abuse is because it will not be for the benefit of the people. It will be for their personal gain. Out of their desperation to accomplish their dreams they will take advantage of those who are loyal to them. That's what happened to the children of Israel when they chose Saul as their king. He used the people for his own benefit. Saul was self-centered.

"And Samuel told all the words of the Lord unto the people that asked of him a king. And he said, This will be the manner of the king that shall reign over you: He will take your sons, and appoint them for himself, for his chariots, and to be his horsemen; and some shall run before his chariots." (1 Samuel 8:10-11)

To make a name for one self

"ÁND THE whole earth was of one language, and of one speech. And it came to pass, as they journeyed from the east, that they said one to another, Go to let us make brick, and burn them thoroughly. And they had brick for stone, and slime had they for mortar. And they said, Go to, let us build us a city and a tower, whose top may reach unto heaven; and let us make us a name, lest we be scattered abroad upon the face of the whole ear. And the Lord came down to see the city and the tower, which the children of men builded. And the Lord said, Behold, the people is one, and they have all one language; and this they begin to do: and now nothing will be restrained from them, which they have imagined to do. God to, let us go down, and there confound their language, that they may not understand one another's speech. So the Lord scattered them abroad from thence upon the face of all the earth: and they left off to build the city." (Genesis 11:1-8)

It would have been OK if they wanted to build more than one city for the people to live in, raise their families and worship God. The original instructions to Adam and Eve were to subdue the earth. In order to do that, they could not

132

stay in one location. God scattered them because their motive was wrong. They wanted to make a name for themselves. The scripture said they had plans to reach heaven. I would hope the bible meant they wanted to build skyscrapers and not attempt to reach the actual heaven where God resides. No one will ever reach God's kingdom with man-made machines or buildings. I am not a building engineer, but I do know that before a skyscraper is erected the builder cannot go higher than the specification of the foundation. The people on the tower of Babel needed to know how high their building was going in order to accomplish their goal. No wonder God came and stopped their foolishness. Some time God has to put a stop to things to protect us from ourselves.

Back in 1977 I met a bishop who was the pastor of a small church. I was new to the Washington, D.C. area and I was looking for a church. The church family was a warm and friendly bunch of people but I couldn't stay because he was pastoring for the wrong reasons. He was consumed with trying to make a name for himself. He practically begged me help him. I did attempt to offer my advice, but that was not what he wanted from me. After all I was only 21 years old. I could tell he was not going anywhere because his motives were wrong. They held service in a large house, what you might call a 'church house'. The first floor was the main sanctuary. It had good potentials. It had a nice porch, but it needed some work. With a skillful handy man, they could have turned that porch into an attractive entrance. The inside also needed work, especially the floors. The pulpit area looked half decent at a distance, but it was a dangerous place to stand or sit. I discovered that first hand when I was asked to preach one Sunday evening. When I finished ministering, I sat down in one of the pulpit chairs and literally fell through it because it had no support. It appeared to be a nice cushioned chair, but it had no support in the bottom. The springs were gone. I became very angry because I almost hurt my self and all he wanted to talk about was being in the league with the other bishops in the city. He went out and bought the biggest Cadillac he could find. He also bought a big hat and the bishop's collars. He did not stop there. Out of his determination to keep up with the other churches he signed a contract with the radio station for a 15 minutes broadcast on Sunday evenings. The church could not afford it so he paid for it out of his pocket. When he got the contract he told me that the people would look at him differently because he was in the league. I attended one of the broadcasts and it was a disaster. If I had known what I was walking into I would not have gone that Sunday. I was in the building when I realized what was going on. Once I was seated his wife asked me to share a testimony over the airway. The service was live and it was horrible. She played a piano that needed to be tuned. In my opinion, it was beyond repair. When they turned the service over to him he did not have message fit the people in the building, let alone for a radio audience. His message had no structure whatsoever. He was so nervous that he stuttered and stumbled all over his words. I was totally embarrassed. That was my last time visiting that church. Not only was this bishop in it for the wrong reasons. The church was unattractive as I discussed earlier. Supposed he had taken all the money he wasted trying to keep up with others and fixed up the building. I only visited them for a short period of time and I was embarrassed to take anyone with me when I went there.

I kept in touch with some of the people who attended the church for a short period of time. I was told of a sad ending for the church and the bishop. His wife became an invalid and the church began to fall apart. The membership scattered because his wife actually carried the church before her health failed. The bishop eventually left his wife because he wanted his freedom to pursue his ministry and other interests. He eventually got sick with cancer and died before her.

We must keep our motive in check as we lead God's people because there are warnings about scattering God's people. (Jeremiah 23:1) We will give an account for everything we do.

CHAPTER 16

LACK OF DISCERNMENT

—⅏—

This chapter has been written to help you understand the gift of discernment. Every Christian should be able to discern spirits in order to know rather they are of God. However, a person's involvement in ministry and their level of maturity will determine how they will use this gift. With the correct application, those whom they serve can benefit greatly.

Discerning of spirits is God's number one way of exposing the enemy so you will know how to deal with him when he comes into your presence. In the scripture below the prophet Elisha operated very accurately in this area.

"Then the king of Syria warred against Israel, and took counsel with his servants, saying, In such a place; for thither the Syrians are come down. And the king of Israel sent to the place which the man of God told him and warned him of, and saved himself there, not once nor twice. Therefore the heart of the king of Syria was troubled for this thing; and he called his servants, and said unto them. Will ye not show me which of us is for the king of Israel? And one his servants said, None, my lord, O king: but

Elisha, the prophet that is in Israel, telleth the king of Israel
the words that thou speakest in thy bedchamber."
(2Kings 6:8-12)

I did a research on the life of Elisha, and I compared him with the other prophets of the Old Testament. I found that he was an ordinary man like anyone else. Although he came from a humble beginning, he increased mightily in his faith. He was set apart because he was willing to go the extra mile. He relied more upon the power of God than others and performed more miracles. Elisha was a very studious prophet while he was in training, and he was faithful in small things. His loyalty and commitment to Elijah far exceeded his fellow prophets. This caused him to move through the ranks and receive a double portion of Elijah's spirit when he was taken from him. The commentators had nothing to say about Elisha's weakness. They only spoke of his strength. To sum it all up, Elisha's life measured up with everything I covered in this chapter.

One might ask, Can a pastor walk in this level of discernment in this 21st Century? The answer is yes. As you continue reading you will find that you must first fix those areas in your life that you can correct so you can freely move into the realm of discernment.

I teach people that they must do first things first. Before you worry about being used by God supernaturally to discern what's going on in some one else's life, make sure you have a handle on your own life. The bible speaks of being faithful over a few things and God making you rulers over many. It also speaks of being trusted with little before you can be entrusted with much. When it comes to operating in the power and anointing of God you must watch out for the little things that others fail to do. It is those little things that will short-circuit your gifts.

Every pastor wants to operate with signs and wonders following their ministry but they must first pass the test. The first test is submitting and understanding to the will of God. In order to master the will of God one must lead a disciplined life and apply sound judgment in his/her day-to-day affairs. Too many folks worry about the will of God but they lack integrity. If you work on your integrity, you will find yourself flowing more smoothly in the Spirit.

There are two forms of discernment: **natural discernment** and **supernatural discernment.** The natural consist of using wisdom that one has learned from years of experience. A good example of this is when you track the life of Abraham. As he walked with God, it is noted that most of his success came from natural discernment. He was an aggressive business man. He obtained this through years of dealing with people. On many occasions he predicted what was going to happen before it happened. This was an example of his ability to operate in the realm of natural discernment. It is nothing wrong with natural discernment. Both of them are necessary, but you must know when to use it and when not to use it. There are times when you must rely upon the Holy Spirit for the supernatural. Natural discernment caused Sarah to believe that she and Abraham were suppose to fulfill God's will through Hagar. It turned out that their decision was incorrect. They were called to rely upon the supernatural because Sarah was past the age of bearing a child on her own strength.

The devil moves in many areas to hinder the growth of churches. Without the ability to discern his movements, we will not know that he has launched his attack.

"My people are destroyed for lack of knowledge: because thou hast rejected knowledge, I will also reject thee, that thou shalt be no priest to me: seeing thou hast forgotten the law of thy God, I will also forget thy children." (Hosea 4:6)

As Abraham and Sarah grew in their faith, they got rid of those things that spoiled their faith. He also learned how to accurately discern what the will of God was. He became strong after many years of trial and error. When God spoke to him about offering Isaac as a burnt offering, Abraham relied solely upon his faith. He discerned that it was the voice of God. He moved on it regardless to rather or not it made sense. His faith was credited for righteousness because he trusted God as being faithful. When he reached the place he left the young men who traveled with them to watch over his donkeys while he and Isaac continued up the mountain for the sacrifice. He said "we will go and worship and come again" because he trusted God to provide.

It is possible for a preacher to have many hang-ups that are stifling his ability to lead a productive life personally. This will also cripple his ability to lead God's people and operate in the gift of discernment when necessary. In order to live productively you must do the following:

1. Seek God first.
2. Have an agenda.
3. Count up the cost.
4. Guide the affairs of the church with discretion.
5. Manage your personal business in a timely manner.

Another hidden attack that devil is using against the human race is generational curses. It is possible that many folks in your congregation are victims of this curse. If it is attached to their lives, they will repeat the failures of their ancestors. As a result they will always find themselves hitting a brick wall or going around and around in circles year after year. I have seen cases where almost every one in the church was defeated spiritually, financially, and emotionally, etc. If the majority of the people in your church are in bondage and you lack the ability to discern what is wrong, your lack of knowledge will serve as your defeat.

Prove all things:

"BELOVED, BELIEVE not every spirit, but try the spirits whether they are of God: because many false prophets are gone out into the world." (1 John 4:1)

I am an instructor at the county jail. One morning I woke up with an inmate heavily on my mind. The first thought that came to my mind that God wanted me to visit him. I had a lot to do that particular morning and it would call for me to rearrange my schedule to fit him in. For a few moments I considered the matter. After a few moments it dawned on me that I could call and see if he was still at the jail. When I called, I was informed that he was transferred. I concluded that it was only a passing spirit who wanted to interrupt my schedule. I prayed for the young man and went own about my business. My point is that every thought that comes across your mind is not always God speaking to you. It could be a passing thought. When a thought comes to you, prove it before you hastily act upon it.

Pastors at War:

"From whence come wars and fightings among you? come they not hence, even of your lusts that war in your members? Ye lust, and have not: ye kill, and desire to have, and cannot obtain: ye fight and war, yet ye have not, because ye ask not." (James 4:1-2)

The priest Eli began to war within himself because he had gotten old and all those things he should have done in his younger years were catching up with him. His personal house was out of order and he had many distractions in his life. He had become dull in his ability to discern. He should have been saturated with the power of God. As he sat upon the seat by the temple post he was observing the people who had come to worship. He misjudged Hannah. (1 Samuel 1-20) He thought she was drunk because he drew his conclusion based upon her body language. We have the same problem in many of our churches today. Some pastor doesn't have the gift of discernment. They rely heavily upon people's body language. That explains how some one can misinterpret a matter.

I work for the Federal Government, and I get all kinds of feed back from people who don't attend church that often. One Tuesday I went to work and an individual who had a bad experience at a church approached me. She was very disturbed over what happened to her. She visited a church, which she described as "a little fiery storefront". She stated that it was different, but she was enjoying the service as she sat quietly in her seat. The most of the people were on their feet clapping and singing. Although being of the Catholic background, she was not accustomed to that form of worship, but she said it was a moving experience. She stated that the pastor pointed her out, made her stand up and made some comments to her about being quiet. He continued to say what God had showed him. She told me that he had her all wrong. Although she was hurt and embarrassed by him she did not want get up and walk out so she decided to stay and keep the program because his phone number was listed on it. She decided to call him to expressed her concerns and explain her self, thinking that her phone call would cause him to be sensitive to others if they visited his church. When she called him to express her concerns he became very defensive and responded that out of the 20 plus years he had been pastoring, he never had anyone to call him and complain about how he operates. She was very angry after the phone conversation with him because she tried to share her feelings in the most respectfully manner as possible, but he rejected her. After that experience she stated that she would never visit his church again because she felt he was arrogant and self-righteous. When she approached me with her concerns, I felt embarrassed. I tried my best to apologize for the experience and soften her feeling about the pastor. I make it a practice not to speak against other pastors. In all honesty, he spoke to her based upon her body language as his guide and not being led by the Spirit. I advise any one in church if you are a prophet you can not use a person's body language to discern spirits. Accurate discernment would have revealed to the pastor why the woman was sitting quietly in the service. As much as possible, I recommend that you leave visitors alone. They will not come around if you are operating in the flesh.

The next example I would like to share is about the old prophet in the book of Kings. (1 Kings 13:1-32) He was dull because he had gotten out of the will of God and he was operating in the flesh. He should have been operating in the office of a prophet like the other powerful prophets we read about. Instead, he was busy listening to gossip. God sent the man of God into the city to condemn the altar. The old prophet should have been doing what the man of God came to do. Just like today, when a person is not where they should be, they will feel threaten and become competitive. When the old prophet could not persuade the man of God to come to his house, he lied to him and said that God had spoken to him too. He was full of deceit. That explains why he could not be trusted. He lost his anointing because his personal life was out of order. The story has a sad ending but it was recorded for our admonishment.

The power of God is available unto every pastor because you have a serious job to do. If you are willing and obedient to the call of God, you will be used to impart understanding to a multitude of people. Pay the price and you will operate in the gift of discernment.

CHAPTER 17

LACK OF ANOINTING

—ɷ—

*"And it shall come to pass in that day, that his burden
shall be taken away from off thy shoulder, and his yoke
from off thy neck, and the yoke shall be destroyed
because of the anointing." (Isaiah 10:27)*

The anointing is a gift from God that enables a person
to carry out an assignment. It is easy for a pastor to get
busy with church work and not operate under the anointing.
The enemy will attempt to yoke them with many forms of
distractions so that they lose sight on the vision and become
burnt out. It is the anointing that eliminates the stress and
strain of trying to make things happen. You must allow
God to use you to your full potential. Once you have been
anointed, you have the responsibility to guard your spirit
because the anointing must be maintained.

The early apostles were men that were highly anointed to
spread the gospel. Although they faced persecution and oppositions, they could not be stopped. The more they persecuted
them the more the church grew. They did not strive against
the anointing, they embraced it and the angels of the Lord
assisted them when matters got beyond their control. When
you are facing persecution, it is not the time to run. You must

stand on God's word and allow the power of God to flow through you. That's what it means to embrace the anointing. It is through the crushing where we get the fresh oil.

What Every Preacher Should Know:

It is more to the anointing than shear luck. It is power of God working on your behalf to confirm that He is with you. When David defeated Goliath it was an easy task because of the anointing. If you study the lesson carefully you will find that David's chances of winning the battle was next to impossible. Goliath was bigger, stronger, and better equipped than he. Goliath biggest problem was that he did not know God, and secondly he was not anointed to fight against David. David's protection was the anointing. That's why he took off Saul's armour because knew that it was not in the sword or the shield.

"Then said David to the Philistines, Thou comest to me with a sword, and with a spear, and with a shield: but I come to thee in the name of the Lord of hosts, the God of the armies of Israel, whom thou hast defied. This day will the Lord deliver thee into mine hand; and I will smite thee, and take thine head from thee; and I will smite thee, and take thine head from thee; and I will give the carcases of the host of the Philistines this day unto the fowls of the air, and to the wild beasts of the earth; that all the earth may know that there is a God in Israel. And all this assembly shall know that the Lord saveth not with sword and spear: for the battle is the Lord's and he will give you into our hands." (1 Samuel 17:45-47)

When David released the stone from the sling, it was the power of God [anointing] that caused the stone to hit Goliath in the right place. It was a miracle because the stone had to get pass the ones that bore the shield who stood in front of Goliath as his protection.

Anointed people are disciplined.

The are two things I want to share about disciplined people:

1. The strength of one's anointing is the ability to use self-control at all times.
2. The strength of ones salvation is not how they perform in church; it is how they live behind closed doors.

When the angel of the Lord announced to Samson's parents about his birth they were given instructions about the disciplinary action they were to take. They were also informed that the child was to be a Nazarite unto the Lord. The anointing lifted off of Samson because he did not maintain the anointing by disciplining himself as instructed.

It is possible to start out as a highly anointed pastor, but if you don't use self-control you will become as others who are powerless. You are on the cutting edge of a great move of God. I challenge you recognize who you are and value your gift. It is not too much for you to handle. It is through the power of God that work is being done.

Anointed people have limitations.

Another reason why some pastors lack the anointing is because they don't understand that with the anointing there come limitations. John the Baptist was assigned to a certain place. He also was on a certain diet and his ministry lasted for a certain period. He knew when to step up to the plate and he knew when to step back.

*"John answered and said, A man can receive nothing,
except it be given him from heaven. Ye yourselves bear me
witness, that I said, I am not the Christ, but that I am sent
before him. He that hath the bride is the bridegroom: but
the friend of the bridegroom, which standeth and heareth
him, rejoiceth greatly because of the bridegroom's voice:
this my joy therefore is fulfilled. He must increase,
but I must decrease." (John 3:27-30)*

In the early part of the twentieth century the United States was introduced to revival known as "The Azusa Street Revival". We can trace most of our Pentecostals, Charismatic, Evangelicals, and etc. directly or indirectly to this revival. From that we had about twelve major evangelists to spring up throughout the U.S. Known as "God's Generals. These men and women attracted large crowds because of the miracles that followed their ministry. This lasted over a 60-year span. During those years many were healed and set free. Most of those evangelists suffered from some form of becoming burnt out before they left the scene because they did not recognize their limitations. No matter how powerful we are, we need rest. We also need to maintain a personal relationship with the Father. In spite of the workload, you can't violate your limitations. Jesus always went to a solitary place to be alone in prayer. He was not so moved by people that he placed their needs above his personal relationship with the Father.

Not every pastor has been called to permanently stay in the position as a pastor of a church. Some are Church Planters or Pioneers who will eventually step back and allow another to carry the work on. It doesn't mean they will quit working for God. It simply means that they will move into the office of a bishop, an apostle or an administrator. Others that are too old to continue to function should recognize when it is time to step back and allow the church to go on. I hear some people say there is no retirement in ministry. That is not true. When a person becomes too old and is dealing with health issues, they need to do the church the courtesy of stepping aside. If pastor is an invalid or in a nursing home the immediate family needs to do the church the courtesy by speaking up and have their loved one replaced so the ministry can go on. I have seen dozens of ministries suffer because the pastor did not know when to step back. On the other hand many large churches are blessed simply because the founder knew when it was time to step back so the anointing could continue to flow through a new leader. Don't miss this, because this is important to the future of the church.

If you build it, they will come.

A movie came out many years ago entitled "If you build it, they will come." It was a movie that had a meaning where in this man built a baseball stadium and for a while he had problems and it seemed like it was not working. In fact it attracted spirits of famous baseball player who once lived.

The movie ended with people coming from miles to visit the field. We too must be determined to have faith and dream. Our first priority is to create an atmosphere for people to come and feel the presence of God. It is no need in thinking that a building is going to do it alone. There are many pretty churches throughout the world but the seats are empty.

We must go back to old fashion fasting and praying. Pray that the empty seats in your church be filled. Let's fast that the people who are staying away from our churches be set free from this yoke. In Isaiah chapter 58 we are taught to fast that we break every yoke. You should fast for two reasons.

1. That Spirit of God is present in your services in a powerful manner.

2. That yoke of excuses are broken off of people when you invite them to church.

When I speak of the anointing I am speaking of the power of God present in your church to perform miracles. You must walk by faith and create an atmosphere for the Holy Spirit to have the freedom to operate.

This generation needs to see something. When many of the Jews came to the tomb of Lazarus and saw what Jesus did, they put their faith in him.

I was teaching in a session and I asked the class how many of them had actually seen a miracle before or how many had witness someone getting healed before their eyes? To my surprise no one raised their hands, including the ministers that were in the class. I personally believe in order for some people to believe, they need to witness what they read in the bible firsthand. Exposure plays a major role in our belief. Lets' examine the following event.

"And one of the multitude answered and said, Master, I brought unto thee my son, which hath a dumb spirit; And wheresoever he taketh him, he teareth him: and he foameth, and gnasheth with his teeth, and pineth away: and I spake to thy disciples that they should cast him out; and they could not. He answereth him, and saith, O faithless genera-tion, how long shall I be with you? how long shall I suffer you? bring him unto me. And they brought him unto him; and when he saw him straightway the spirit tare him; and he fell on the ground, wallowed foaming. And he asked his father, How long is it ago since this came unto him? And he said, Of a child. And ofttimes it hath cast him into the fire, and into the waters, to destroy him; but if thou canst do any thing, have compassion on us, and help us. Jesus said unto him, If thou canst believe, all things are possible to him that

*believeth. And straightway the father of the child
cried out, and said with tears, Lord, I believe;*
help thou mine unbelief." *(Mark 9:17-24)*

The first problem in the above passage is that the disciples could not heal the boy because they had not experienced this level of demon possession before. They were given power over evil spirits to cast them out, but they had never encountered anything of this magnitude before. The second problem was that the father of the boy had an emotional attachment to the boy that interfered with his faith. That's why he said "help thou mine unbelief." It is possible that you can unconsciously hold onto a level of unbelief. It is based upon what you know. Jesus in the story was able to break through the barrier for the man and his disciples by performing a miracle.

As a pastor you must build a place of residence for your congregation to reside in, and not allow their faith to rest upon enticing words of men's wisdom but in demonstration of the Spirit and power of God (1 Corinthians 2:4)

If your church lacks the power of God in your midst, you can't continue to live in denial. We are operating without the anointing. It is amazing how much American churches accomplish without the power of God. I am talking about the power that we read about in the book of Acts. Most large churches are growing not because there is demonstration of the power. They are growing because they have the manpower and resources to appeal to people's emotions. At the same time most people in the world with medical problems attend church on a regular basis. They are not healed because they are programmed that way.

Let us pray that miracles return back to our churches. It did not die with the apostles. Nor did it fade out with the pioneers of the twentieth century.

Miracles have at least three major purposes:

For The Benefit of The Recipient

- God is concerned that our needs are met. (Matthew 7:11)
- A miracle sustains our faith; because it from faith to faith we grow. (1 Peter 2:2)
- It gives those who will examine us after a miracle, something to hold on to. (John 11:36-37)

For The Benefit of The Disciples

- The disciples were students and they needed to understand that the power of God was not limited, no matter the situation. (Matthew 8:23-27)
- Miracles caused the disciples to follow Jesus with an intense desire to be like him. (John 6:68-69)
- Miracles caused the disciples to put into practice what they learned from Jesus before he was taken from them. (Acts 2:42)

For The Benefit of The Church Today

- Miracles close the doors of doubt. (Daniel 5:12)
- Miracles are the greatest witness that Jesus is the Christ. (Luke 7:16)
- Miracles cause people to become miracle minded. (Acts 5:15-16)
- Miracles will provoke the church to demonstrate what was done for them or what was done before their eyes. (Acts 4:13)
- Miracles enhance the believer's prayer life. (Acts 6:3-4)
- Miracles promote church growth. (Acts 5:14)

- Miracles cause people to give. (Acts 4:32-35)
- Miracles will cause a person to reverence God and His people. (Acts 5:11)
- Miracles encourage people to make sacrifices. (Act 4:37)
- Miracles will enhance the way a church worship. (Acts 3:8-9)
- Miracles will establish a reputation in the community wherein the church will be looked upon as a pillar of hope. (John 4:30)
- Miracles will separate you from people that don't mean you any good. (Acts 5:13)
- Miracles will crush the stony hearts of unbelievers. (John 11:45)

CHAPTER 18

LACK OF PROFESSIONALISM

—ɯ—

I know a lot of folk think we are fools for Christ, but in all truth, we are supposed to be the most intelligent group of people in the world. The fact that we are called fools, doesn't mean that we are actually crazy. We just appear crazy to some because we live by faith principles and we worship God.

We live among professionals, and when we operate in gross ignorant, it is a bad reflection on the body of Christ, and it tarnishes our witness. We are never to compromise the gospel to fit in, but we are supposed to be wise as serpents.

Many churches can't attract people who are wealthy or business minded because the people of the world have a better standard of living than that of many Christians who goes to church faithfully.

It will serve those who lack professionalism to seek training in Church Etiquette and Social Etiquette. We should be a light to the world when we hold events in public places.

I believe that when a church holds a banquet, it should be a time of celebration, but it should also be a time of evangelism. Your program should not be so churchy and radical that until you appear to those who observe your event as unprofessional.

I attended a celebration recently and the music was of poor quality. They sang songs that were not appropriate for ministry to church groups let alone to the unchurched. This event had a large group of people that catered the food. They were a potential harvest. The program was not in the best of interest to them. The church group carried on so unprofessionally until I was embarrassed to be among them. To make matters worse, the guest speaker made a racist remark. When he did that, it changed the atmosphere in the room for the remainder of the day. If he had only paused for a second and scanned the room before he made the statement, he would have noticed that there were various ethnic groups among the servers and the guests.

When you go out to various events, you should operate with grace and elegance. You should focus on attracting new people to your church at all times. That is what I call "The Ministry of Excellence."

Keep in mind, when you are at a funeral, wedding, banquet or any special event you should be thinking evangelism. You should be on your guard because when people come to a gathering, they are seeking something. That may be your only chance to minister to them.

"The fruit of the righteous is a tree of life; and he that winneth souls is wise." (Proverbs 11:30)

Nebuchadnezzar was the greatest world leader in the bible because he knew how to select the right people to help him build his empire. When he captured Israel, he brought only the best people into the land of Babylon. The rest of the people were left in Israel with a ruler over them. Daniel and the Hebrew boys, had the aptitude for learning astrology and literature. Although Daniel and his companions came into Babylon as captives, they purposed in their hearts that they would not defile themselves. For that reason they, set the standards for others to live by. In spite of persecution, they gained much respect because they were professionals who would not compromise.

"As for these four children, God gave them knowledge and skill in all learning and wisdom: and Daniel had understanding in all visions and dreams. Now at the end of the days that the king had said he should bring them in, then the prince of the eunuchs brought them in before Nebuchadnezzar. And the king communed with them; and among them all was found none like Daniel, Hananiah, Mishael, and Azariah: therefore stood they before the kind. And in all matters of wisdom and understanding. That the king inquired of them, he found them ten times better than all the magicians and astrologers that were in all his realms." (Daniel 1:17-20)

Jesus was also a professional when he walked the earth. As a child he knew how to sit among professionals and hold an intelligent conversation.

"And Jesus increased in wisdom and stature, and in favour with God and man. (Luke 2:52)

When a church is criticized for the lack of professionalism, they usually view it as persecution. The real truth of the matter suggests that when that happens, the church provides the ammunition for the attacker to use against them. It is a better witness for God by being classified as people who are professionals than to be labeled as unprofessional.

CHAPTER 19

UNATTRACTIVE SANCTUARY OR MEETING PLACE:

—ɯ—

S mall churches are meeting in all kinds of spaces because they cannot find an affordable place to set up a permanent house of worship. Finding a space can be a challenge depending on what city you live in. Some cities have available space but the ministries are too poor to afford them. In other locations they have the money but there is a shortage of rental property suitable for a church. Others are running into difficulty finding spaces in shopping centers because some landlords are no longer interested in renting out their space to church groups because they can make more money renting out to a business rather than renting to a church. Lastly, but not leastly, some churches have made it hard for others by burning their bridges, and now the landlords are unwilling to deal with another church group because of a bad experience.

For those who are fortunate to find space in a shopping centers, please don't become an eyesore. The church should be professionally decorated. The days for poorly hung drapery are unacceptable. When a church set up in a business complex, it needs to blend in with the color scheme and pattern of the fellow businesses. If all of them have mini blinds at their windows, that is what you should use. It is a bad witness when the unchurched look upon a storefront church with little respect because of poor decoration. There are some churches that has big windows but are in need of a major make over. Some have old snake plants that are kept in mismatched pots in the window. They have seen their day and they look like something that someone brought off their back porch. If you are going to use live plants, they should be maintained weekly. You can become immune to things that others are turned off by.

You will need to spend money on the outer appearance of the site. It doesn't always take a lot of money. In most cases, all it takes is a fresh coat of paint and new carpeting to make the place look attractive.

On one occasion we arrived early for bible study. The room that we were using was small but my oldest son wanted to arrange the chairs differently. When he got through the entire atmosphere changed. When I stood up to teach there was a burst of energy in the room. It was a small change, but it did wonders.

The outside church sign should be big, professionally done and in uniform with the rest of your neighbors in the shopping center.

Those who meet on school property need to watch out for things that can possibly work against them. They should decorate the space and create an atmosphere that it is a place of worship. If they meet in the cafeteria, they should use air fresheners to get rid of the smell of sour food or dirty mops. If a church is not sensitive, they will become immune to the unpleasant odors and think nothing of it. A visitor will pick it up as soon as they walk in the door. Have someone spot-check the bathrooms and flush the toilets that are left untidy. Some school custodians will work closely with churches, while others will not pay any attention to your efforts. Please note that this will be a reflection on you instead of the school.

(It is the small foxes that spoil the vine) If the custodians are out right sloppy, you will need to meet with the principal's office and resolve your issues.

Customer Service

Wal-mart basically dominates most department stores because of customer service and good prices. When a person gets to Wal-Mart it is a one-stop deal because they carry everything under one roof. Small churches must strive for the same goals. A church should be a place fully equipped to meet the needs of the whole man.

Years ago storefronts were very attractive because they were fiery, they had good music and they had good preaching. Many of the traditional churches were dead. For that reason the storefront churches attracted many folks.

Today, many traditional churches have come out of their boredom, they have better music and their services are very attractive. Many of them have also improved on the appearance of their building. To top all of that, many traditional churches have hired trained ministers who are better preachers.

If a person has a better choice, they will probably choose the beautiful traditional church that is conveniently located at the end of the street. Since traffic is posing major problems in many cities, neighborhood churches are attracting more people than before. People have better selections of churches to chose from before they visit a church who hold service in the school or storefront. In order for them to chose a storefront or school that, church it must become very attractive spiritually and physically.

This chapter was not written to discourage you but it has been written to put strong emphasis on the fact that is up to you to make your meeting place attractive. You will attract people because there are still those that want to be in a smaller setting. You don't want it to be said that the visitor was turned off by the appearance of the building.

CHAPTER 20

UNORGANIZED

—∽—

If a pastor is out of order and unorganized in his personal business, it is a good possibility that he will run the church the same way. Once a person gets their personal business in order, the church will flow much smoother.

Since Sunday services attract the most people, it is advisable that your services have structure. This is important because as I stated before the first eleven minutes are crucial for a ministry if you are striving to impress first time visitors who are looking for a church home.

I would like to address praise and worship because visitors have to go through that phase of the service before they get to hear the sermon. Praise and worship is ministry. Keep in the mind the presence of the Lord only shows up when He is pleased with the people who are attempting to provoke His presence. Where the spirit of the Lord is there is liberty. It is possible for people to be healed and delivered in that portion of the service. Praise and worship also create at atmosphere for the ministry of the word. If that doesn't take place the messenger is going have to work harder because the climate is not right. There are two important things to remember:

1. If the praise and devotional leaders are untrained they may be running people straight out of the door.

2. If your team can't get along or their personal lives are not measuring up with the ability to sing, it is not worship, it is abuse.

Suggestions for Praise and Worship:

1. In order to be an effective praise and worship leader, the person(s) should lead a life style of praise and worship.
2. They can't prepare for leading a worship service only minutes before the service takes place.
3. They should have weekly rehearsals and decide who is going to be the key worship leader in the service.
4. They can't be busybodies into everybody's business in the church.
5. They should be consecrated for the assignment because worship is a form of warfare.
6. Use a jubilant praise or a short praise melody as an opener to attract the audience.
7. Worship should be inviting and attractive to your audience without verbally rebuking or insulting them for not participating to your expectation.
8. Once you get in front of the people, don't leave the platform or praise area.
9. It is intimidating if the church is small, you have visitors and your worship leader starts walking down the aisles and putting the microphone to someone's mouth. That takes the person's mind off of God. It will cause them to worship the worship leader.
10. Don't force people to read their favorite scripture or give a testimony.

11. They should have enough songs in case they need them.
12. Don't mix all kinds of songs.
13. If you are singing about the blood and you have related songs keep them in order so you can flow from one to the other.
14. If you are singing hymns follow a pattern, and gradually move into a higher praise.
15. Sunday mornings are not the best time to introduce your audience to new songs unless they are easy or it is only repeating what the lead person is singing.
16. If it is a new song and it's easy, make sure all the folks on the praise team know it to help facilitate the transition.
17. One way to introduce a new song is to present it when you have bible study.
18. Once the people are in a worship mode, don't jump back to singing praise songs.
19. Pay attention to your audience; don't close your eyes for long period of time as if they are not there.
20. If you notice that people are looking out the window, folding their arms, began to sit or they have stopped singing, it is a good possibility that you are boring. Don't rebuke them. It is a sign that the praise leader needs to sit down.
21. There are times when you need to invite people to sit while you continue with the worship service. That will make them feel like you are considerate of the fact that they have been standing a long time.
22. Be sensitive when visitors come in, especially if they are unchurched. They like to hide in the crowd and if your church is very small, they already feel like they are on the spot. **Leave them alone!**
23. Don't ask parent to put toddlers down and get up and praise the Lord if they are sitting down holding

a big child while praise service is going on. You may be asking for trouble because that child may be a roamer and when the pastor gets up, they are not going to want to sit down.

24. If you have screaming children and they are practically taking over your service you may consider starting a nursery among the young mothers of the kids. This will ensure that you have coverage to rotate on Sundays and everyone will enjoy the services.

Altar Workers:

A side from having a new member's class or orientation, you need to have trained staff members to assist with new converts. Some churches are not prepared when people join the church in response to a salvation appeal. You cannot assume that they are going to automatically return to the next service. This generation needs to be mentored into the fellowship.

If you plan to keep the people who responded to the altar appeal, you need to assign a staff to one or two persons. The following list provide some things your staff should do when working with new converts immediately after they leave the altar:

1. Make sure they have a medium size notebook for information purposes **only** such as phone numbers and notes on the person.
2. Introduce them selves and welcome the new converts to the family of God.
3. If they accepted Christ at the altar, make sure they understand what they did. If they don't understand but are serious about salvation, clear up their understanding and read to them Romans 10:8-13 and lead them into the sinner's prayer again.

4. Don't take anything for granted. Be aggressive but not bossy. Go the extra mile to get them to safety.
5. Walk in faith at all times.
6. Talk about the importance of coming to church. Don't leave it up to them as to what to do next. Close all doors that don't need to be opened.
7. Don't send them to the church of their choice, talk about your church. (New babies goes home with the parents)
8. Call them within the next 48 hours.
9. Pray with them after each conversation.
10. Talk with them about water and Spirit baptism.
11. Don't push people off on the pastor. However; if you come across a problem that the pastor needs to be aware of, make it your business to bring it to his attention.

Confusion

The reason I added to confusion to this chapter is because unorganization can cause a lot of confusion in a church.

"For God is not the author [a God] of confusion,
but of peace, as in all churches of the saints."
(1 Corinthians 14:33)

If God is not the author of confusion then Satan is the author of confusion. He can take a little confusion and keep a church in turmoil. Many of our large as well as small churches are filled with it. One problem after the other has wounded a large number of people. There are thousands of people that have stopped going to church because they were wounded. Most of it is minor, but when we don't communicate the devil turns an anthill into a mountain.

God is orderly. If you are going to attract and impress outsiders you must be more like God. In doing so, you must become organized. A church is not suppose to be a place where any thing goes. All through bible history you can read about organized events. Listed below are 15 events that were detailed and impressive.

1. The creation of the heaven and the earth. Genesis 1:1-31, 2:1-3
2. The specification of the ark. Genesis 6:14-22
3. The specification of those occupying the ark. Genesis 7:1-16
4. The unloading of the ark and the first public sacrifice. Genesis 8:15-21
5. The attempt to build a tower [skyscraper]. Genesis 11:1-9
6. The burial of Jacob. Genesis 50:1-13
7. The specification of the tabernacle. Exodus 25-27
8. The high priest vestments. Exodus 28-29
9. The altar of incense. Exodus 30
10. The invasion of Jericho. Joshua 3-4
11. David brings the ark back to Jerusalem. 2 Samuel 6:12-19
12. The preparation and building of the house of the Lord by Solomon. 1Kings 5-7
13. The preparation of Temple by David. 1 Chronicles 22:2-19
14. Erection of the temple. 2 Chronicles 3-5
15. Elijah returns the people back to true worship. 1 Kings 18:30-30

Tardiness:

One big turn off is to have your guest waiting for your worship service or related events to get started. When you run late because the church doesn't have it together, it is hard to convince people that they should be apart of what you are doing. The only persons you will attract to your ministry will be people who are always late themselves. That's why we hear the familiar term "Birds of the same feather flock together". If you keep attracting late people, it will only add to the stress level and it will become a breeding ground for confusion.

I would like to share some tips when you are hosting a special event or a fund-raiser. Make sure you have committee to discuss the event from start to finish. Practice makes perfect; you don't want to come cross as a bunch of unorganized folks. If you have a deliveryman delivering fixtures or equipment for the event, please allow extra time in case he gets lost or stuck in traffic. It may be worth it to get your equipment a day or two early because this will allow extra time for individuals who will be operating it time to get familiar with it. If you need to assemble items, make sure you have individuals who can test them out in advance and become expert at assembling them the day before the event.

CHAPTER 21

ABUSIVE AND CONTROLLING MINISTRY

—◊—

S ome pastors have gotten out of the will of God because they are abusing the people whom they are responsible for. They have not been good and faithful stewards over the flock that they have been entrusted with. Below I have provided a parable showing when a servant is not faithful over what he has been placed in charge of, it will be taken from him and given to those who will treat them right. That is what's happening to some pastors. The membership is being taken from them and given to the pastor that has the larger church because they are faithful. They should not get upset with a pastor because their flock joins a larger ministry.

"Take therefore the talent from him, and give it unto him which hath ten talents. For unto him which hath ten talents. For unto every one that hath shall be given, and he shall have abundance: but from him that hath not shall be taken away even that which he hath." (Matthew 25:28-29)

The next passage makes it plain that the church does not belong to the pastor. It belongs to God. As you serve you should have a servant mentality and you should also keep in mind that you should be an example. Last but not least, you should not ask people to do what you are unwilling to do. Your congregation is your investment. You must equip [feed] them in every area of their lives so that they can be well nourished. They should not go around like beggars seeking to be fed by another ministry because they are not being fed at home.

"Feed the flock of God which is among you, taking the oversight thereof, not by constraint, but willingly; not for filthy lucre, but of a ready mind; Neither as being lords over God's heritage, but being examples to the flock. And when the chief Shepherd shall appear, ye shall receive a crown of glory that fadeth not away." (1 Peter 5:2-4)

Although pastors should delegate assignment to the congregation, they should make it a rule never to pass off their dirty work on those who are loyal to them. When David sinned against Uriah, he abused those around him, including Uriah. He tried to use them to cover his tracks and do his dirty work after he found himself in a dilemma.

Another problem in small churches is eavesdropping. When a church is small many pastors can't help but know what's going on with people in the congregation. Don't waste time attacking people with information you stumble across. It is not discernment. It is abuse. It is ok if someone brings something to your attention that needs addressing. However, it is not good to have a tattle tail in the church. When a pastor gets into using this activity, it becomes a breeding ground for manipulation and psychology. No one grows from it.

Draining ministry

Another form of abuse is when a ministry is overbearing on the congregation by taking too much away from their family; draining them of their time and money. If you hold too many services during the week and require the same members to be present at everything that's going on at church, you are you abusing them. Another sure way to drain your congregation is to schedule more than three preaching engagement per month with other churches, plus a heavy in-house church schedule.

Small churches cannot follow large churches. A large church can afford to keep their doors open every day because they don't have the same people involved in all the activities.

A wise pastor will study his congregation's potential and not drive them. He should not compare them with another congregation. When you praise their ability and not pressure them, they will began to participate with excitement towards the vision that you have set forth.

If you gather information from conferences, seminars and other related training that will enhance the ministry, make sure you don't take on more than the people can handle. If you notice that the people are stressed or overwhelmed about a project, make adjustments to lighten the load. This will let them know that you are sensitive to their feelings.

When you are fundraising, rehearse it in their ears that you only want them to do their best and don't worry about what they cannot do. You need to also make them aware of the importance of keeping the right attitude about giving when they don't have any money to give.

Please treat men like men, women like women and youth with respect allowing them to be youth. To sum up what I am saying, don't treat grown-ups like kids. Especially, if they make a mistake about something. Correct people in a positive manner.

We live in a time when some groups have gone overboard with ministry gifts. When a church has thirty members and twenty-eight of them are wearing some kind of ministry title and about ten of them are prophets, some thing is wrong with that picture. Especially when the turn over rate is high and less than three people joined the church in the past year.

When a small church has dozens of prophets, they will think there must be a prophecy in every service. They will have a tendency to want to run folks' lives, telling them when to quit jobs, where to live, who to marry and, etc. There is no way that God is going to tell me who to marry through a prophet and neither the potential bride or myself know anything about it. God doesn't operate like that. The main function of a prophet in this hour is to confirm what the Spirit is saying to the individual. Keep in mind we are in the dispensation when the Spirit of God dwells on the inside of every believer. The Old Testament prophets [seers] were used to reveal to the people what to do in most cases because there were no open visions. In this hour we are under the New Testament era. For that reason the responsibility level for the prophet is different. If a so-called prophet doesn't know the difference between an Old Testament prophet and a New Testament prophet, that person is going to abuse everyone they attempt to minister to.

I am not against the ministry of the prophet. I am against error. When prophets are overbearing, they cripple people and it leaves them thinking that God don't speak to people individually. Every Christian should be able to hear the voice of God for themselves. There comes a certain level of independent when it comes to being a successful Christian. Please note the following scripture.

"God Who at sundry times and in divers manner
spake in time past unto the fathers by the prophets.
Hath in these last days spoken unto us by his Son, whom
he hath appointed heir of all things. By whom also
he made the worlds." (Hebrews 1-2)

When a so-call prophet scares people into staying at a church that they no longer wants to attend, it is abuse. They usually have individuals fearing that they are going to die or get sick if they leave. In all honesty they are going to die if they stay.

Some pastors take matters into their hands that are not their business. I recall a pastor telling his congregation that he was not giving out any tithes report for the year because they should be giving their money to God and not giving it for the sake of tax benefits. Those who do that are out of order.

As I prepare to close this chapter, I would like to share an example of how King Saul placed the people under fear and caused them to faint. This is a good example of the King putting his personal desires above the needs of the people.

"And the men of Israel were distressed that day; for Saul had adjured the people, saying, Cursed be the man that eateth any food until evening, that I may be avenged on mine enemies. So none of the people tasted any food. And all they of the land came to a wood; and there were honey upon the ground. And when the people were come into the wood, behold, the honey dropped; but no man put his hand to his mouth: for the people feared the oath. But Jonathan heard not when his father charged the people with the oath; wherefore he put forth the end of the rod that was in his hand to his mouth; and his eyes were enlightened. Then answered one of the people, and said, Thy father straitly charged the people with an oath, saying, Cursed be the man that eateth any food this day. And the people were faint. Then said Jonathan, My father hath troubled the land: see, I pray you, how mine eyes have been enlightened, because I tasted a little of this honey. How much more, if haply the

people had eaten freely today of the spoil of their enemies which they found? For had there not been now a much greater slaughter among the Philistines?"
(1 Samuel 14:24-30)

CHAPTER 22

POVERTY DRIVEN MINISTRY

—◇—

When Moses returned to Egypt to rescue the children of Israel and free them from slavery, they were also enslaved in their minds. With a strong and mighty hand God delivered them and caused them to walk out of Egypt. When they arrived at Mt. Sinai God established His covenant with them as an attempt to stabilize them so they could go on and possess the land. At that time He set up guidelines for living, which they were commanded to bring the first fruit of their crops and the first born of their livestock as a sacrificial offering. As I studied His plan of giving throughout the bible, it points to the fact that giving is an act of faith and it serves as a reminder to the people of God that He is our source. Lastly, it should keep us aware of the fact that everything we have belongs to Him.

Tithing is God's ideal plan for financing the ministry. However, it is sad that less than ten percent of the Body of Christ give like they should. For that reason leaders have to come up with ways to generate funds in order to balance the church budget.

The Jewish people had to resort to taking a temple tax in Jesus' day because the funds were not coming in like it should. When they approached Peter about paying taxes, Jesus sent him fishing to miraculously generate funds.

The first approach to generating funds is for the pastors to teach on tithing and giving because some folks have a misconception about giving. Many of them are afraid to give because they are struggling to make ends meet in their homes. The following passage serves as our foundation for giving.

"Give, and it shall be given unto you; good measure, pressed down, and shaken together, and running over, shall men give into your bosom. For with the same measure that ye mete withal it shall be measured to you again." (Luke 6:38)

"Honor the Lord with thy substance, and with the firstfruits of all thine increase: so shall thy barns be filled with plenty." (Proverbs 3:9-10)

"Will a man rob God? Yet ye have robbed me. But ye say, Wherein have we robbed thee? In tithes and offerings. Ye are cursed with a curse: for ye robbed me, even this whole nation. Bring ye all the tithes into the storehouse, that there may be meat in mine house, and prove me now herewith, saith the Lord of hosts, if I will not open you the windows of heaven, and pour you out a blessing, that there shall not be room enough to receive it." (Malachi 3:8-10)

"Every man according as he purposeth in his heart, so let him give; not grudgingly, or of necessity: for God loveth a cheerful giver." (2 Corinthians 9:7)

"Be not deceived; God is not mocked: for whatsoever a man soweth, that shall he also reap. For he that soweth

to his flesh shall of the flesh reap corruption: but he that soweth to the Spirit shall of the Spirit reap life everlasting."
(Galatians 6:7-8)

Personal Experience:

When I first started the church that I presently pastor. I did not think about a building fund for the first few years. I thought I was doing the people a favor by not asking too much of them. As time went on I started noticing that the money I was saving my people they were giving it to other ministries. If you don't ask and set goals, the people will think that all is required of them is to give two dollars when you pass the offering plate.

During that period I visited a few banquets and large events. I began to notice that people were going to conferences, camp meetings and concerts. They were not afraid to spend large sums of money. Not only were they attending these events, they were paying for other folk. They bought products such as videos, cds, cassettes and etc. They also bought items for their friends who were not able to attend. After noticing this I made up my mind to generate some income for the ministry of my own. Today I take a special building fund offering once a month. I promote various forms of fundraisers and sell our ministry products. After I woke up, our building fund made a complete turn-a-round. Suppose I had known better from the beginning.

People need to be taught to expect to receive for their giving. You should also teach them to give their praise reports when God blesses them. This will confirm to the others that giving works. There are people that are afraid to talk about their blessing because there are those who can't stand to see others with wealth. Those that get upset over someone's financial blessing are in bondage with a poverty spirit.

The reason why some folks don't get a kick back on their giving is because they have bad habits when it comes to managing their finances. You can confess all kinds of prosperity scriptures. But if you are wasteful and living above your means you are not going to see those scriptures at work on your behalf. The same holds true for healing scriptures. You can confess them but if you violate your body you can expect to be sick.

Generating funds:

When you have a fund-raiser don't take on projects that are bigger than your ability to handle because it will overwhelm your congregation. That's why you should plan very wisely. Once you discover what works best for you, use it to the glory of God. Some churches will condemn other churches for selling dinners or other related projects. Those who sell dinners are no different from those who are selling recordings of their services. Soliciting a person as a faith partner is also a fund-raiser. In all honesty, faith partners are taking money from many small churches because most partners attend small churches.

A pastor had a member in his congregation who had a pledge card from another ministry boldly displayed on her dining room table when he got there to pray for her. She pledged $1,000.00 to this Television Evangelist. This person was not a tither at her church and had never given over $20.00 in an offering at any time since he was there. I believe every person should to do their best for their own church before they make pledges to other ministries. After all, he visited her on several occasions at the hospital and responded to her family every time they called him. The person she gave the pledge to do not know she existed and he eventually fell into sin and is no longer on television.

When you use the following fund-raisers always look for ways to promote the gospel.

1. Car washes
2. Musicals
3. Shopping trips
4. Talent shows
5. Fashion shows
6. Bake sales
7. Yard sales
8. Dinners
9. Donuts or candy sales

While you may use some of the above fund raiser, a large ministry will use the following ways to generate funds:

1. Conference registration
2. Book Store
3. Tape ministry
4. Faith partners
5. Faith and seed offerings
6. Special Offering gifts
7. Building Use (banquet halls)

I am not against the large or small churches in their effort to generate funds as long as they are upright in their deeds and are not taking advantage of people.

We have hundreds of churches that are not getting anywhere when it comes to owning property. Every ministry should have a building fund. If you live in a metro are such as Washington, DC, you are in multi-million dollar arena. You need to seriously look ahead and realize that everyone is getting old and if you don't do something to accommodate the future of your ministry, old age and health issues will caught up with you.

Managing a church is not all spiritual. You have a natural responsibility to sit down and count up the cost. Counting up the cost means developing a plan of action.

Among many Christians I am finding that many of them don't own anything from a personal stand point. This explains why some churches can't get off the ground. When people don't own much, they have difficulty seeing the need of generating thousands of dollars. They are accustomed to living from pay check to pay check and without coaching you won't get them past two hundred dollars when you are working on a fundraiser.

If too many people in your congregation are struggling, it is up to you to get help for them. This will make them feel good about the church. Members can benefit from seminars or information such as:

1. Homeownership
2. Getting out of debt
3. Credit repairs
4. Resumes and job seeking skills

Another problem that I have cited is that many churches are spending too much money on rent and advertising. If you are only taking in four thousand dollars a month, you don't need to be renting a two thousands dollars a month store-front. Whatever you rent, your monthly rent should not be more than the amount you take in each week. If not, you are managing the church from a paycheck to pay check concept. You should seek to keep more of your funds if you plan to have something. If a church is not saving at least three thousand dollars a month towards purchasing their own property they are in for a rude awakening.

"For which of you, intending to build a tower, sitteth not down first, and counteth the cost, whether he have sufficient

to finish it? Lest haply, after he hath laid the foundation,
and is not able to finish it, all that behold it begin
to mock him, saying, This man began to build,
and was not able to finish." (Luke 14:28-30)

It is necessary to sit down with a Finance Manger or a Loan Officer and find out what it will cost to build a church. Once you understand what is required, you will need to go through a process of elimination. Eliminate everything that you are doing that is ineffective and draining the church of its funds. I wasted a large amount of money advertising on the television, radio and various types of mail outs. Since none of these efforts brought in a positive response, I got rid of them.

Jesus did not waste time on those that did not receive him. He returned to his home town and preached the gospel. The people did not respond. He was only able to heal a few folks. Jesus went on from there to other places where he was productive.

Many churches have been on the radio or television only to discover that it didn't attract any new growth nor did they gain any financial support from the listening audience. It only took away from the ministry, costing thousands of dollars that could have gone into the building fund. Keep in mind most non-believers don't listen to Christian radio or television programs. In fact there are a large number of so called Christians who listen to the Jazz and rock stations when they are at work.

You must test your out reach efforts. If you go on the radio and your attendance doesn't increase or your listening audience doesn't support you financially, **Wake up. You** are throwing money out the window.

Let's face facts. Every one is not radio and television material. It takes a special charisma, voice and correct approach to appeal to the listening or viewing audience.

I don't mean any harm, but a pastor with broken English, southern accent or poor bible knowledge and does not know how to appeal to the listening audience need to come off the radio. On rare occasions you will find a pastor who is operating in signs and wonders and his audience will overlooked his poor broadcasting skills.

In every major city there are about ten pastors that dominate the radio audience. If you are not in that league, you are not going to gain from it. You may think it's not fair but that is how it is. The same holds true for Christian authors if you are not known, no body is going to buy your books until you come up with a plan. Once an author is among the best sellers they can write anything and it will sell.

The nationally known preachers are selling enough products to pay for their programs. They are getting richer while the unknown pastor is heading for bankruptcy.

I have provided a break down to summarize what I have discussed in this chapter. It shows how much money some ministries are wasting. If you are renting and don't have a decent building fund going, you are wasting money if your program is not causing church growth or paying for itself.

Break Down:

If you have a weekly broadcast and are spending $800. 00 per week:

In one month you have spent $ 3,200.00
In six months you have spent $19,200.00
In one year you have spent $41,600.00
In ten years you have spent $416,000.00

You figure, if you have less than $10,000.00 in your building fund account and you have been on the radio for ten years, you were not paying attention. The money you wasted in broadcasting could have been a down payment.

Some pastors are afraid of being called greedy so they don't ask for special offerings to provide for what they are trying to accomplish. I heard a pastor say he only take one offering during the week because he don't want people to criticize him for being in ministry for money. He is on the radio and holds service in a storefront. If he doesn't wake up and prepare for the future of his ministry, it is going to catch-up to him. I want to pass the baton one day and its my desire that the next pastor of my church will walk into a debt free ministry with everything he needs to function. Joshua was a good warrior, but not a good leader because all he accomplished died with him.

You may not be able to do all you would like to do. I recommend that you move in phases. Get started towards better. Before I was able to buy a single family home, I bought a town home. When I earned enough equity I was able to buy a single family. God is waiting for you to make your move. He has a miracle waiting for you.

CHAPTER 23

DULL BECAUSE OF SIN

—ᴍ—

The Struggling Preacher:

Keep in mind that sin is defined as missing the mark and any form of it will slowly drain anyone regardless to who they are. Satan knows how to use sin to short-circuit a Christian's relationship with the Father and if he succeeds they will become dull. Some pastors are dull because they are struggling with sexual sins. Satan targets this area because there is a level of guilt that comes with sexual sins that stains the conscience worse than other acts of sin. I thought it was needful to address this matter because we are constantly facing embarrassment. Godly men and women are caught up in unchasetened behaviors in the body of Christ. We are losing a large number of church workers, youth pastors and senior pastors because of sexual sins.

Studies have revealed that about 90% of Christian men struggle sexually. In addition to being a pastor of a church, I am a prison minister and a mentor. All these areas of ministries have placed me in a position to deal with a wide scope of men. Due to the fact that many of them have sought my help in their struggles, I conclude that the findings are accurate. Most men feel threatened because they don't know what their normal response to human sexuality is.

Until they get a grip on themselves and have a good relationship with God they may walk around feeling guilty. A man with a good relationship with God will process human sexuality better than a man who is carnal or those who lacks understanding. Another reason why some men are stronger than others is because they are careful to obey God's word and uses a higher level of integrity. They carry themselves in a discreet manner with a controlled chain of thoughts. My point is, if they are close to God they will think about sex, but it will only be a passing thought. It is when a person is not close to God and doesn't use discretion is when it will become a lingering thought pattern. That is the reason why many are led down an unhealthy road of sexual impurity.

I am not saying that the discreet man is inhuman because all men think about sex. That's a part of our manhood and there is nothing wrong with a man who can't keep his hands off his wife, who enjoys sex with her on a regular basis. I also want to share that there is also nothing wrong with young or old men who have questions on their minds about human sexuality for the purpose of educating themselves.

Thoughts alone don't mean that a man is lustful. A person has not sinned if the thought of sex runs through his/her mind. It is when those thoughts turn into lust and it has conceived. A lustful life style determines perversion. You are lustful if you are lusting after someone who is not your spouse. If a person lusts after the same sex, are involved with pornography, a child, an animal or are always daydreaming about an orgy, they fit the description of a pervert and are displeasing in the sight of God.

Periodically, I deal with those who confide in my counsel because they want to be free. Below, I have provided a frequently asked question and statement that men seek my advice on:

Question: Why is it, that when I have practiced sexual sins and stand to minister, it seems like I am flowing in a heavier anointing? There are other times when I struggle and refrain from sinning and fast to consecrate myself, yet when I get up to minister, I stumble and feel less anointed.

Answer: When a man indulges in sex, something happens to his ego mainly because it is a sense of fulfillment and most gratifying to the flesh. He feels a sense of achievement, whether he is a husband with his wife or a violator of God's law. The achievement will pump up his adrenaline.

It is disturbing to know that a large number of preachers and gospel singers are performing off their adrenaline and emotions. When they hit the pulpit or the stage it seems as if the heavens have kissed the earth. The devil will confirm that it is all right to continue in their sexual secrets because it didn't affect the anointing. Remember that he is a liar. Some folks are good not because they are anointed, they are good because they have practiced and they are simply good at what they do. You must also be-aware that your audiences are human beings, emotional beings and spiritual beings. The latter is not always ministered to because many Christians settle for being entertained instead of being ministered to. Ministry is supposed to challenge a person and provoke change while entertainment only brings temporary relief because it only appeals to one's emotions.

To answer the last part of the question; the reason you feel less anointed is because you have placed more emphasis on your performance rather than on your relationship with God. Christian men should practice fasting to keep themselves subject to the Spirit and not led by the flesh. The chosen fast will loose the bands of hidden sin, namely sexual sins. It will undo the heavy burdens of trying to perform. Fasting will free you from the oppression of a guilty conscience. Last, but not least, fasting will break the yoke of constantly repenting for the sin you have been struggling to get free from but have not been successful. Bondage is when you try to get free but can't free yourself. I will also add that the person who feels less anointed when he fasts and struggles to stay pure is very sensitive because he is in and out of sexual sins. Once he comes to terms with his walk with God, takes a stand and stop basing his accomplishments on his feelings, he will stop stumbling. He will accurately flow in the anointing and it will be confirmed with signs and wonders. Sinners will also be convicted when they are in the audience.

There is a difference between the anointing and appealing to one's emotions. Emotions will only excite your audience but there is no power present to deliver them. It is the anointing that destroys the yoke (Isaiah 10:27). I often remind people that they cannot take people where they have not gone.

In this hour older men are falling into sexual sins just as much as younger men. My advice to older men is to beware because the devil will come again with the struggles of your youth. As you get older you must accommodate your age.

You cannot become too busy and wear yourselves down without renewing yourselves daily. You must not lose focus on who you are and you must also keep in mind that you need to become a role model for younger men. Although you are not as young as you used to be, you should be wiser as you get older.

My final advice to older men is to use self-control and stay close to God so that you will remain sharp and you will stay ahead of the devil. When he shows up with his old tricks, you will be prepared. It is true that as we get older our bodies change. These changes will impact your sexual ability, and mood swings. It is important to understand that your relationship with the Lord will empower you to deal with mid-life and your senior years.

Pastors Under The Microscope:

The reason why some pastors play around with sin is because they are talented and it has gone to their heads. Any time a person is not where he needs to be he has a tendency to abuse his gift. They will use charm and psychology on people. This is done through control and manipulation. I will use David as an example, when he got ready to sin by committing adultery, he used the authority of his position to set everything up. He used and abused people that were loyal to him to help him carry out his lustful desires.

For those who are struggling with sexual issues, please note the following:

The anointing to preach and sit in the office of a pastor is a supernatural gift. However, when a pastor is lukewarm or burned out, he will become dull and live above the law. If he had a background of sexual struggles, it is a good possibility that he will become very vulnerable all over again and Satan will deceive him.

I must reinforce what I said earlier, this sin heavily impacts the conscience, which works on the person's confidence. When a person's confidence is low, their faith has no energy to it. When they are depleted in their faith, their self-esteem crumbles. When that happens they get away from their assignment to seek fulfillment in the wrong areas and when they are walking down this slippery road of temptation, they will slip.

I like to use examples when I say things to let you see that it has happened before. All that Satan will do is what he has done before. Here is my previous character, David. This time I would like to share a clearer picture.

And it came to pass, after the year was expired, at the time when kings go forth to battle, that David sent Joab and his servants with him, and all Israel; and they destroyed

*the children of Ammon, and besieged Rabbath. But David
tarried still at Jerusalem" (2 Samuel 11:1).*

David knew in advance that this was going to happen. It was not a coincidence that he stumbled on a woman bathing herself within view. It appeared to be premeditated. He conveniently stayed at home while sending everyone else off to war so he could carry out his fantasy. David was a great strategist. Because he was carnal, he used his abilities selfishly. In his calculation, he knew when Bethsheba would come to bathe. He had seen her there before because he kept an accurate record. He committed adultery and attempted to use his skills to cover his sins. Although he had gotten over on people he was too dull to recognize that what he had done displeased God. He could not prosper in the situation because he was out of order.

Our God is merciful. He sent the Prophet Nathan to David to expose his sins so it would bring conviction and lead him to repentance.

Above everything else you are a holy vessel. You must watch your life of association because you are sanctified. You must know that the devil will lead you astray if you don't stick to your assignment.

Married or single, you must stay alert to maintain your spiritual strength. Samson messed-up because he failed to stick with the assignment. He was supposed to be strong every day that he woke-up.

One way to avoid the pit-falls of sexual sins such as: masturbation, pornography, and other forms of fornication, you are to do more than just enough to get by. Jesus told his disciples to pray lest they enter into temptation. The spirit is willing but the flesh is weak. The flesh enjoys sexual sins; however, it is nothing spiritual about it.

I plead with those who are in the body of Christ and are guilty of the above discussion to repent like David and get your house in order, because as long as you continue in this manner you will not prosper. When a pastor operates in sin and rebellion, it leaves his church vulnerable to the attack of the enemy.

"Or else how can one enter into a strong man's house, and spoil his goods, except he first bind the strong man? And then he will spoil his house." (Matthew 12:29)

The Process:

In the beginning of this chapter I stated that one must repent and the strength to do right will start flowing. That is true but some people may need help along the way. For those who find themselves needing help. Please study along carefully and work your way into victory over the flesh.

The flesh is weak.

"Watch and pray, that ye enter not into temptation: the spirit indeed is willing, but the flesh is weak.""
(Matthew 26:41)

Knowing that the flesh is weak is an alert to let us know that we cannot take anything for granted but that we must stay on our guards. The scripture teaches what shape the flesh is in, but we can become spiritually strong and overcome it. Keep in mind a weak body will become subject to a man that is spiritually strong. It only controls those who are spiritually weak.

Be strong in the Lord

"Finally, my brethren, be strong in the Lord, and in the power of his might." (Ephesians 6:10)

In order to become strong in the Lord one must submit to the Lordship of our God. You must also proceed to become educated about who our God is, respect and agree with his godliness. You must study about Him and how He dealt with those that we read about in the bible. Last but not least, you must become educated about who is your enemy and know your rights.

I know you may not feel like studying all that is provided in this chapter but once you have read through this book I challenge you to come back and study along with an open bible. Below I have provide three outlines to help you process what it means to be strong in the Lord.

1. Temptation

"There hath no temptation taken you but such as is common to man: but God is faithful, who will not suffer you to be tempted above that ye are able; but will with the temptation also make a way to escape, that ye may be able to bear it." (1 Corinthians 10:13)

Study guide:

1. Matthew 26:36-46
2. Ephesians 6:10-18
3. James 1:1-15
4. Genesis 22:1-19 (The word "tempt" in this chapter means to test)

Points to ponder:

1. Jesus defeated the devil because he was prepared.
2. Jesus prayed until he got his break-through.
3. Jesus took his disciples with him into the garden to teach them how to prepare for a test.
4. While Judas was in the temple making a deal – Jesus was in the garden praying.
5. Judas was in the right place but doing the wrong thing.

What to do about this weak body:

1. Become spiritually strong.
2. Put on the armour of God.
3. Separate natural fights from spiritual warfare and fight in the right realm.
4. Set boundaries for yourself by living by these principles:
   a. Live truthful (trustworthy).
   b. Live righteous.
   c. Live a peaceful life.
   d. Live by faith principles.

Reinforce your life with the following:

1. Make sure you are a Christian by God's standards.
2. Make sure you study the bible and apply what you learn.
3. Make sure you pray for yourself and others with understanding.

What to do about temptations:

1. When you are in a test, go all the way through it.

2. Make sure you stay in the will of God at all cost.
3. Come to a mature decision why you should not complain.

2. God

"But seek ye first the kingdom of God, and his righteous-
ness; and all these things shall be added unto you."
(Matthew 6:33)

Scripture reading:

"And he gave some, apostles; and some, prophets;
and some, evangelist; and some, pastors and teachers;
For the perfecting of the saints, for the work of the ministry,
for the edifying of the body of Christ; Till we all come in the
unity of the faith, and of the knowledge of the Son of God,
unto a perfect man, unto the measure of the stature of the
fulness of Christ: That we henceforth be no more children,
tossed to and fro, and carried about with every wind of
doctrine, by the sleight of men, and cunning craftiness,
whereby they lie in wait to deceive; But speaking the truth
in love, may grow up into him in all things, which is the
head, even Christ: From whom the whole body fitly joined
together and compacted by that which every joint supplieth,
according to the effectual working in the measure of every
part, maketh increase of the body unto the
edifying of itself in love." (Ephesians 4:11-16)

God brings good out of evil

*   Genesis 50:19-21
*   Job 1:1

God access to

- Psalms 145:18
- John 14:6
- Hebrews 4:16
- James 4:8

God, Creator

- Genesis 1:1
- Nehemiah 9:6
- Psalms 24:1

God, grace

- Romans 3:24
- Romans 11:5
- Ephesians 2:8
- 2 Peter 3:18

God, holiness of

- Exodus 15:11
- Leviticus 19:2
- Habakkuk 1:13
- Revelations 4:8

God, love of

- Isaiah 54:10
- John 3:16
- John 17:23
- Romans 8:31

God, sovereignty of

- Exodus 18:11
- Psalms 93:1
- Psalms 95:3
- Matthew 6:10
- Romans 14:11

3. Know who is your enemy:

THE DEVIL AND DEMONS

- Where did the devil come from? (Isaiah 14:12-15; Revelation 12:7-10)
- The devil (Satan) is a fallen angel. (Isaiah 14:12; Revelation 12:7-10)
- The devil was once named Lucifer. (Isaiah 14:12)
- The devil cannot enter in and out of heaven as he wishes. (1 Corinthians 15:50)
- The devil rule in the power of the air. (Ephesians 4:2:2)
- The devil does not own the earth. (Psalms 24:1)
- Every Christian is stronger than the devil if they will stay close to the Father. (Luke 10:17-20; Romans 8:31; 1 John 4:4)
- The devil cannot possess a Christian. (Mark 3:27)
- A backslider has the capacity to house many evil spirits in his body and/or mind. (Matthew 12:43-45)
- Demons are fallen angels that were deceived by Satan. (Matthew 25:41; Jude 1:6; Revelation 12:7-11)
- All demons may not appear to be evil. (Acts 16:16-18)
- Hell was made for the devil and his angels. (Matthew 25:41; Rev 12:7&9)

- The devil is not in charge of hell. (Matthew 25:41; 2 Peter 2:4; Revelation 20:1-3; Revelation 20:10)
- The devil has not been to hell yet. (Job 1:7; Revelation 12:9&12; Revelation 20:1-3; Revelation 20:10) [To cast the devil out and send him back to the pit are vain words.]
- The devil did not have the keys. (Revelation 1:18; Revelation 9:1-3; Revelation 20:1-3)
- The keys the bible refers to are keys of authority, not physical keys. (Mat 16:17-19; Matthew 18:18-20)
- Jesus did not have to go to hell to take the keys and release the innocent. (Matthew 27:50-54; John 19:30; 1 John 3:8)
- When the scriptures refers to Jesus being in the heart of the earth it was referring to the tomb and not hell. (Matthew 12:40)
- Heaven or hell are not on the same sphere that planet earth exist on. According the bible, they appear to be parallel to each other but far apart. (Luke 16:19-26)
- Jesus died in victory and a proclamation went out on earth. (Matthew 27:51-54)
- A proclamation went out in hell to the spirits in prison [Jude 1:6] and not innocent people. (1Peter 3:19)
- Not all demons are loosed. (Jude 1:6)
- The demons that are loosed are only loosed for a season. (Matthew 8:29,31)
- There are divers forms of possession. (Matthew 9:32-33; Mark 5:1-20; Luke 11:14; Luke 13:11)
- Some spirits control territories, known as territorial demons (Ephesians 6:12)
- There is such a thing as demonic activities. (Daniel 10:12-13; 2 Corinthians 12:7)
- There is such a thing as demonic oppression. (1 Samuel 17:14; Mark 5:1-20)
- Listed below are seven major type of strongholds:

1. Anger, rebellion, bitterness and un-forgiveness.
2. Sexual perversion – homosexuality, molestation, child pornography & incest.
3. Witchcraft, Occultism & Generational curses.
4. Poverty.
5. Physical affliction.
6. Depression &Fear (timid and drawback reactions).
7. Laziness (procrastination, wasting time [idol] and always changing one's mind).

Jesus Our Example:

Jesus was not dull; he was sharp. No one could get over on him or entrap him in the least manner. As I strive to become all that I can be as pastor in this 21st century, I keep my focus on my favorite hero – Jesus Christ. Jesus would not conform to this world but in stead he was transformed by renewing himself daily. As you ponder this section of this book, may you desire to be like Jesus.

When Peter came in the house, Jesus spoke first.

"And saith, Yes. And when he was come into the house, Jesus prevented him, saying, What thinkest thou. Simon? of whom do the kings of the earth take custom or tribute? of their own children , or of strangers?" (Matthew 17:25)

He would not entrust himself to any man.

"But Jesus did not commit himself unto them, because he knew all men. And needed not that any should testify of man: for he knew what was in man." (John 2:24-25)

He said, "thou have spoken truthfully."

*"The woman answered and said, "I have no husband."
Jesus said unto her," Thou has well, I have no husband:
For thou hast had five husbands; and he whom thou now
hast is not thy husband: in that saidst thou truly."
(John 4:17-18)*

He asks this only to test him.

*"When Jesus then lifted up his eyes, and saw a great
company unto him, he said unto Philip. Whence shall we
buy bread, that these may eat? And this he said to prove
him: for he himself knew what he would do." (John 6:5-6)*

When he heard that Lazarus was sick.

*"When Jesus heard that, he said, this sickness is not unto
death, but for the glory of God, that the Son of God might
be glorified thereby." (John 11:4)*

In concluding this chapter I would like to focus on the examples that Jesus displayed in the above passages. He moved in power and authority from start to finish. That is why he could shout "it is finish" and drop his head and die on the cross. No one took his life. He gave his life and he died on schedule. Finally, I admonish you to live your life to the full extent of your ministry and don't allow the enemy to tempt you. Sin will only cause your life to become dull and you won't finish in victory.

CHAPTER 24

THE UNBALANCED CHURCH

—ɯ—

It is often stated that individually we are the church and not the building itself. For that reason when I speak of the unbalanced church, I am speaking about the individuals who need to become settled in God. We live in a time when the world is out of control. Therefore, if we are going to reach them, we must become balanced in our conduct.

Please note that Abram in the book of Genesis, eventually became a solid man of God. It did not happen over night. As he began walking with Him, he had to become deprogrammed and reprogrammed God's way. It was through trial and error that he got himself together. He was not living in poverty when God called him to move out of the land of Ur. He was successful. The only thing he lacked was how to completely trust God. That is how you measure success. By the time Lot left him, Abram was very rich and striving for perfection. His entire household was blessed because of his obedience to the Father.

Too Close To The Edge

We often speak of how God blessed Abram after he and Lot separated, but not too many folks mention that it was not good for Lot to leave Abram in the first place. Abram offered him a choice but he did not protest like Ruth did when her mother-in-law suggested that they should separate. Without counting the cost, Lot left Abram the first chance he got. Out of greed and selfness he chose the best of the land and left his uncle with the poorest of the land, but through a miracle God blessed him in spite of what Lot did to him. He did not realize it would have been better for him to sell some of his livestock and stay close to his uncle and say like Ruth, "Entreat me not to leave thee, or return from following after thee: for whither thou goest, I will go; and where thou lodgest, I will lodge: thy people shall be my people, and thy God my God: where thou diest, will I die, and there will I be buried: the Lord do so to me, and more also, if aught but death part thee and me. (Ruth 1:16-17) If he didn't want to sell some, he could have set up feeding stations and send out hired servants to care for his flock. That was a customary thing during bible history when there was not enough grass for the animals to graze upon.

It was because of Abram's balanced life that Lot's life was spared on two occasions after their separation. Please note the following passages:

"And when Abram heard that his brother was taken captive, he armed his trained servants, born in his own house, three hundred and eighteen, and pursued them unto Dan. And he divided himself against them, and he and his servants, by night, and smote them, and pursued them unto Hobah, which is on the left hand of Damascus.
And he brought back all the goods, and also brought again his brother Lot, and his good, and the women also, and the people." (Genesis 14:14-16)

Suppose Abram was living too close to the edge and had not prepared himself by training his servants in the event of an attack. All he would have been able to do was to weep and mourn for his nephew Lot.

"And he said, Oh let not the Lord be angry, and I will speak yet but this once: Peradventure ten shall be found there. And he said, I will not destroy it for the ten's sake."
(Genesis 18:32)

God spared Lot the second time. This was only for the sake of Abram. If it weren't for him, Lot and his entire family would have been destroyed when the wrath of God fell upon Sodom and Gomorrah without having a clue as to what hit them.

Many pastors are like Lot. They started out with much more than they are left with, but because they are not together and unbalanced, they are constantly losing instead of gaining. Pastors must follow God like Abram did and not do like Lot. Lot lived too close to the edge. That is why he was not growing. When a person lives like that, they live only for the moment and not considering the value of a long-term commitment. We should live a disciplined live and count up the cost daily. Those who compromise their intimacy with God for fame and fortune will reap the repercussion of failure that is just around the corner.

Too Far To The Right

Another example of an unbalanced church is to become so rigid in your thinking until you think you are the only one that is right. I call it "Too Far To The Right." Don't allow the spirit of segregation to stifle your growth. Don't see other pastors as a threat to your ministry. If you hold services near a community, there is enough people in less than a five square mile radius to pack out your church three times and over. There is no reason to be jealous over someone else's success.

In the following verses, Jesus reminded his followers of being too far to the right.

"And John answered him, saying, Master, we saw one casting out devils in thy name, and he followeth not us: and we forbad him, because he followeth not us. But Jesus said, Forbid him not: for there is no man which shall do a miracle in my name, that can lightly speak evil of me. For he that is not against us is on our part." (Mark 9:38-39)

"And other sheep I have, which are not of this fold: them also I must bring, and they shall hear my voice; and there shall be one fold and one shepherd." (John 10:16)

"And it came to pass, when the time was come that he should be received up, he steadfastly set his face to go to Jerusalem, And sent messengers before his face: and they went, and entered into a village of the Samaritans to make ready for him. And they did not receive him, because his face was as though he would go to Jerusalem. And when his disciples James and John saw this, they said, Lord, wilt thou that we command fire to come down from heaven, and consume them, even as Elias did? But he turned, and rebuked them, and said, Ye know not what manner of spirit ye are of. For the Son of man is not come to destroy men's lives but to save them." (Luke 9:51-56)

Heaven is a beautiful place. It is interesting to know that there will be people from all nations and nationalities worshipping the one God in unison.

CHAPTER 25

VICTIM OF THE SMALL CHURCH SYNDROME

—ɯ—

Every church that I have been involved with was small. I am victim of the small church syndrome. Although I have been victimized, I am not stuck. I have always been a dreamer, but I did not notice that my background had a grip on me that kept me back. Everyone will not realize this syndrome because they are comfortable, and they think it is normal. For that reason, when a person is involved in something and if it is all they know, it is not always easy to determine that it is a problem. What some deem as safe is not always safe. For this reason the cycle can prove to be difficult to come away from. It depends on the person's mindset and how they process what they have discovered.

Let's face it, when a person grows up in a small church everything they do is small and for the most part they are a victim of the reaction I discussed earlier:

1. Low self esteem
2. Negative thinking
3. Intimidation
4. Insecurity
5. Draw-back reactions
6. Stuck-up reactions
7. Naïve about the operation of a large ministry

If a church has twenty members and if only ten of them show up for worship, it will put a damper on everything that will take place that day. Every thing they do will have the word "little" tagged onto it.

1. Little prayer
2. Little song
3. Little testimony
4. Little offering
5. Little sermon

By the time everything is over, every one will feel small. So they will take their *little* selves home.

Some small congregations are attacking large ministries charging that they are snobbish or arrogant. If it is true, don't add fuel to the fire by commenting about it across the pulpit. This will only keep the body of Christ divided. Keep in mind, we reap what we sow. I recommend that you adopt a pastor of large ministry and pray for him/her daily. Don't be a negative thinker and quoting that a haughty spirit comes before a fall. I know that is a scripture, but we need large ministries. I make it a point to pray for every ministry, large or small. I was grieved to hear a fellow pastor comment that he looking for a particular nationally known pastor to fall because he felt that he has gotten too big. That bothered me because I don't want to see any minister fall. Every time something happens to a minister, I feel the pain because we are a part of the same body. If a pastor finds him self rejoicing over another pastor's failure, think on the following scriptures:

"Wherefore let him that thinketh he standeth take heed lest he fall." (1 Corinthians 10:12)

"For the body is not one member, but many. If the foot shall say, Because I am not the hand, I am not of the body; is it therefore not of the body? And if the ear shall say, Because

I am not the eye, I am not of the body; is it therefore not of the body? If the whole body were an eye, where were the hearing? If the whole were hearing, where were the smelling? But now hath God set the members every one of them in the body, as it hath pleased him."
(1 Corinthians 12:14-18)

The Parable of the Talents

A parable is an earthly story with a heavenly meaning. Jesus often used them when he addressed the crowds. There were times when no one knew what he was talking about because he spoke in mysteries. He spoke in parables that his disciple may know what he was saying. I have used the following parable to describe the size of churches and to illustrate what is happening among them.

"For the kingdom of heaven is as a man traveling into a far country, who called his own servants, and delivered unto them his goods. And unto one he gave five talents, to another two, and to another one; to every man according to his several ability; and straightway took his journey. Then he that had received the five talents went and traded with the same, and made them other five talents. And likewise he that had received two, he also gained other two. But he that had received one went and digged in the earth, and hid his lord's money. After a long time the lord of those servants cometh, and reckoneth, with them. And so he that had received five talents came and brought other five talents, saying, Lord, thou deliveredst unto me five talents: behold, I have gained beside them five talents more. His lord said unto him, Well done, thou good and faithful servant: thou hast been faithful over a few things, I will make thee ruler over many things: enter thou into the joy of thy lord. He also that had received tow talents: behold,

I have gained two other talents beside them. His lord said unto him, Well done, good and faithful servant; thou hast been faithful over a few things, I will make thee ruler over many things: enter thou into the joy of thy lord. Then he which had received the one talent came and said, Lord, I knew thee that thou art an hard man, reaping where thou hast not sown, and gathering where thou hast not strawed: And I was afraid, and went and hid thy talent in the earth; lo, there thou hast that is thine. His lord answered and said unto him, Thou wicked and slothful servant, thou knewest that I reap where I sowed not, and gather where I have not strawed: Thou oughtest therefore to have put my money to the exchangers, and then at my coming I should have received mine own with usury. Take therefore the talent from him, and give it unto him which hath ten talents. For unto every one that hath shall be given, and he shall have abundance: but from him that hath not shall be taken away even that which he hath." (Matthew 25:14-29)

Five Talents

This servant went out immediately and traded his talents and doubled it. That tells me that he was not a procrastinator. The five talents represents the mega church, 15,000 and above membership. Some of these churches started within someone's home. Others started with a few hundred people and it grew into a mega church. Which ever occurred, they are to be commended. They have a story to tell. One thing they will tell you is when someone say "no" it's not the end of the world. A procrastinator will sit down, but a go-getter will go and knock on the next door.

Two Talents – Mega Church

Like the above servant, this servant went out immediately and traded his talents and doubled it. The two talents represent the mega church, 3,000 to 7,000 memberships. These churches are productive in the community. Not only are they providing spiritual support, they impacting the communities economically.

Went and Traded

Both of the above servants got up and went to work. They may not have known as much as the servant that had a lot to say, but they were men of action. Knowing something and talking about it don't get anything done. The scripture states that "whatsoever you <u>doeth</u> shall prosper".

One Talent – Small Church

The minimum would have been to put the money in the bank and let it earn interest. He didn't do that. What he thought was enough to get by with was unacceptable. I always remind people that when they do just enough to get by, they always lose. Receiving one talent did not have to be bad. Every hero of the bible started out as one but they went on to accomplish what God chose them to do. I challenge every pastor not to give up. You are on the cutting edge of the next move of God. Get off the fence and get to work. Fence sitters are people who have all the answers but the best they can do is to sit there, watch others, identify their mistakes and criticize them.

Went and Dug in the Earth

Why on earth would someone dig a hole and bury his talent? In order to properly have faith you must line your thinking up with God's word. You can say you believe but if your thinking has not changed you are only speaking out of your mouth but not actually believing in your heart and watching your seeds turn into plants. It is time to renew your mind because the best is yet to come.

I Knew You Were a Hard Man

When bitterness set in a person's heart they will see God as being hard. They will also take it out on others and will not speak peaceable to them.

It was obvious that he had an attitude. This man reminds me of Cain in the book of Genesis. That's the main reason why his offering was not accepted. His attitude play a major factor in everything he did. He had several opportunities to correct his ways and reap the blessings of the Lord. His unwillingness to conform to the will of God led from one thing to the other. He found himself leaving his family and living as a vagabond. For those who think God is hard and He is requiring more of you than others, I challenge you to humble your self under the mighty hand of God.

I Was Afraid

God did not give us the spirit of fear; He gave us power, love, and a sound mind. Fear has torment. When a person is in torment he will misinterpret what is true. When the master of the servant returned, there should have been nothing to fear. His fears held him as a prisoner. He felt alienated from what was meant to be his heritage.

Thou Wicked and Slothful Servant

The man with the one talent proved to be lazy. He should have used his hands, his mind and all his being to cause his dreams to come to pass. He could have turned his situation completely around. No one was in his way to stop him. He allowed himself to be hindered by his thinking. Nothing displeases God more than a preacher that once walked in authority, and now they have abandoned the faith. And now he is speaking all manners of doubt. Don't abandon the faith because the world is dying. You must see the lost as top priority or else you will see no need to invest in those that are helpless.

For Every One Who Hath

I cannot emphasize it enough; there are over 6 billion people in the world. What are you doing about that number?

Are you dreaming about a large church? What are you doing about it? Many pastors are daydreaming that somebody is going to donate some land to them and somebody is going to give them a large sum of money. To add to the dream, they are also dreaming that a church is going to split and a large group of people is going to join their church. It is possible for God to cause a miracle to happen for you, but in order for Him to bless you, you must get involved and prove your self faithful. If you don't accommodate where God desires to take your church, you will see the opposite. The donations and people you were dreaming about will go to the pastors that already have a large church.

From Him That Hath Not

The devil is vicious. I think what distracted some folks is when the bibles introduced the devil; it described him as being subtle. (Genesis 3:1) For that reason some folks treats him like he is harmless. He is never to be treated that way. He must be resisted and not given any space. The reason why the man with the one talent lost out is because the devil confused him. His entire concept of being a faithful servant was twisted beyond measure. He was completely out of harmony with the other servants. That tells me that instructions that were given to them were not confusing. It simply boiled down to the fact that he did not want to conform.

CHAPTER 26

MOST CHRISTIANS DON'T KNOW WHAT TO DO WITH THEMSELVES WHEN THEY ARE NOT IN CHURCH

—⟁—

Christians are a very special group of people, especially, those who are in the age group ranging from the age of 18 to 35. Please allow me to quickly justify my self. This age group is next in line to take this country forward as the older generation is moving off the scene. They are God's chosen, but the devil is seeking to destroy them. They are being targeted because the future of this world lies within their hands. May this chapter open every one's eyes to the devil's schemes.

The baby boomers are divided into two groups. The older group has already retired and is facing health issues. They are also consumed with medical prescriptions and its high cost. The younger of the group is consumed with trying to stay young, but at the same time they are counting down to their retirement. The cares of this world and enjoying one's self is high on everyone's list, therefore many are unaware of the lateness of the hour.

The younger generation (teens and pre-teens) are watching and they are thinking, "being grown-up is cool" so they can't wait for their turn. Satan's ultimate goal is to wipe all of us out. He is cunning but this chapter will expose him who has planted seeds. He planted them while we were occupied with other things. The bible describes it as sleeping.

"But while men slept, his enemy came and sowed tares among the wheat, and went his way. But when the blade was sprung up, and brought forth fruit, then appeared the tares also. So the servants of the householder came and said unto him, Sir, didst not thou sow good seed in thy field? From whence then hath it tares? He said unto them, An enemy hath done this. The servants said unto him, Wilt thou then that we go and gather them up?"
(Matthew 13:25-28)

Before I get too far into this chapter, I want to get back to today's young adults and challenge them to sense the urgency of the time that we live in. Too many of them are only consumers and not producers. They are living from one paycheck to the next. That seems to be the trend of this society, but I want you know it is not the way they should be living. Some young adult go to church to be entertained and that's about it. That is why most youth leaders and youth pastors are exhausted. They are trying to keep today's youth and young adults occupied and interested in church. If this generation is not sold out to God, those who are trying to entertain them is going to run out of ideas and become burned out. That's why I have placed the challenge before them to get involved and take a stand for God. If they will stand long enough it will cause an epidemic and we will see large numbers of young adults becoming serious about their relationship with God.

Today's young adults are looking for fun and seeking to find out how much they can get away with and still be a Christian. I don't like that because it doesn't sound good. Their past time consists of:

1. Hanging out at the malls.
2. Hosting sleepovers and movie nights.
3. Performing in dance and drama ministries.
4. Trying out restaurants late at night.

I am not saying that young adults should not have leisure time to enjoy their friends. There should be time for a personal relationship with the Lord. We should have limits because it is our responsibility to reach the lost.

It is also sad to see that many of our church going youth and young adults are getting killed and arrested. People who go to church commit some of the worst crimes. Many of them are out of control.

When they are challenged about their lack of attentiveness to God's word they will say that bible study is boring. I hate to say it but when young Christians tell me that bible study is boring, I question their relationship with the Father. Especially when I know that the churches many of them attend have experienced and qualified instructors.

It is very harmful to live as a Christian and have very little knowledge of the bible. There are people in our churches today who are holding office and have been in the church most of their lives yet they are full of fear because they are void of God's word. There are basic things we should know after being in church for a while. It is also scary to find that an alarming number of older people don't know the bible at all. I have provided a list of seventeen things that a Christian should be familiar and know where it is found in the bible or at least what book it is found in. Some Christians don't know if these scriptures are in the Old or New Testament.

Things you should know:

1. The Creation. Genesis 1:1-31
2. The Story of Adam and Eve. Genesis 2:1-25
3. The Story of Abraham and Sarah. Genesis Chapters 12-31
4. The Story of Isaac and Rebekah. Genesis Chapter 27
5. The Story of Joseph. Genesis Chapters 37-50
6. The Biography of Moses. Exodus Chapters 2-3
7. The Ten Commandments. Exodus 20:1-26
8. David's Anointing. 1 Samuel Chapter 16
9. The Story of Job. Job Chapter 1-2
10. The Shepherd's scripture. Psalms Chapter 23
11. Tithing. Malachi 3:8
12. The Birth of Christ. Matthew 1:18-25; Luke 1:26-49
13. The Lord's prayer. Matthew 6:5-16
14. Jesus washes his disciples' feet. John 13:4-17
15. Holy Communion scriptures. Matthew 26:17-30; 1 Corinthians 11:23-24
16. God is Love. John 3:16
17. The main scriptures used to lead someone to salvation. Romans 10:9-10;1 John 1:9

After reviewing the above list I challenge you to devote some time to educating yourself biblically. You should be able to hold a discussion on any one of them because they are very common stories in the bible.

Things you need to know and do:

1. Each day you should confess that you have perfect health.

2. Each day you should confess and stir up the gift of faith over your life.
3. Each day you should confess and stir up salvation and joy over your life.
4. Each day you should confess and stir up whatever area of ministry you are involved in.
5. As Children of light, your actions should reflect your faith.
6. It is important to avoid any pleasure or activity that results in sin.
7. Jesus is more concerned about our walk than our talk.
8. Your private life is what will determine whether or not you will go to heaven.
9. Weeds (unbelievers) and wheat (believers) must live side by side in this world. God Will eventually separate them.

Thing you need to know that will eat away at your faith:

1. Your thinking
2. Daily habits such as:
   a. always late
   b. always forgetting things
   c. short patience
   d. always trying to take the shortcut
   e. always whining or complaining
   f. always assuming
   g. always trying to beat the system
   h. selfishness
   i. excessive worrying
   j. always changing one's mind
   k. low self-esteem
   l. timidity
   m. always looking too deeply into things

     n. hung up on justifying your deeds
     o. naiveté
     p. lack of aggressiveness for God's word
     q. lack of self-control
     r. unforgiving

3. Sin
4. Fear
5. Unbelieving society
6. Lack of Prayer
7. Lack of Understanding

We cannot totally blame the people in the pews for where the body of Christ is today. The blame has to be shared. Those that have gone on before us have digressed. I have digressed. We all have digressed. We have substituted the power of God for talents. Talents and gifts are needed in the church but without the power of God they are worthless.

When I was growing up our past time consisted of socializing but it was secondary to evangelism. We spend most of our time grooming our relationship with the Father and introducing young people to Christ or challenging those who were not active in their churches to get involved in reaching our cities. It was normal to see young men and women who were teenagers or those who were in their early twenties standing up as powerful ministers in the late 60's and early 70's. We had a citywide choir and a Youth for Christ movement wherein we traveled to neighboring cities and States putting on citywide crusades and parades. We went door to door passing out tracts and witnessing. We held street services in the worst neighborhoods.

One day we went to a rough neighborhood and one of the youth ministers was preaching a fiery sermon when an angry man showed up. He threaten us and demanded that we leave from in front of his door because he said he was going inside to get his gun and we better be gone when he got back. He further stated if we did not leave he was going to blow our brains out. I was new at doing street service so I was ready to close down and leave but the young minister that I was with was very bold. He turned and looked at the man and said, "We are not going no where you may as well sit down and shut up" and he spun back around to the audience and continued his fiery sermon. I was scared because both of us were youth. To top it off we were small built men and the guy doing the preaching was shorter than me. The man went violently into his house and stayed a few minutes. While he was gone I decided to get caught up with my brother and not let fear get the best of me. I concluded if I am going to get killed I may as well die in the faith and not in fear. The man swung the door open, came out and sat on the stoop. He listens to the rest of the sermon. When we made an altar appeal he was the first one in the line with his hands lifted unto God with tearing flowing down his face. I needed that experience because it did not get any better as we continued to go into the streets. We won many young people to the Lord during those days.

On another occasion we went to a different city and the resistance was very strong. I almost lost a couple of fingers because some one slammed a heavy door in my face. Another youth was threaten in a parking lot and someone attempted to hit her with his car. That young lady was my age and she was very bold. She was responsible for reaching over one hundred youth by her self. Later she won a "go getter" like herself and between the two of them they were responsible for approximately one thousand youth.

Today's church is not as miracle minded. When I came along it was an insult to ask an older person in church for an aspirin. Everybody had a bottle of oil and if you were sick they laid hands on you.

My mother did not attend the same church I attended but she came to my church often and she was exposed to us using oil, praying over the sick and watching them get healed. There were times when she got sick in the night and she awaken me several times to pray for her. I was still in high school but I was armed and dangerous when it came to praying for the sick. One night she came to my bed and woke me up because she was seriously ill. She spoke only above a whisper because of the pains. I had not been sleep that long because I had come in late from church. I rolled over and rebuked the sickness off of her and rolled back into my position and went back to sleep. I was so tired until I honestly don't know how she got back to her room. When I woke up for school, she had cooked breakfast, sent my father off to work (who was un-aware of what had happened) and she was doing the laundry when I went to catch the school bus.

Twenty years before my mother passed away, I was living in Falls Church, Virginia. I was a newly wed and 21 years old. I received a phone call that she was gravely ill. My sister who was with her said things did not look too hopefully. I was on my way to a revival service before the phone rung. After I hung up from my sister I went on to church. I was in a revival assisting the pastor of the church that I was in fellowship with at the time. That was the last night of the revival and he told me to go home to my mother.

My family and friends around the country were all praying for her. There were times when I thought the worst but I kept thinking about the many times when God healed her while I was living at home. I called the airport, made reservation and was on the first flight for Savannah Georgia. Having to change planes and lay over in Atlanta, I did not get to the hospital until late that Saturday afternoon. One of my brothers met me at the airport and he filled my in on my mother's condition which had not improved. When I got to the hospital things did not look good, in fact my mother looked much worse than what I expected. She was in the intensive care with several machines around her and some type of tent over the upper part of her body. I was still armed with my little bottle of oil. When they allowed me to see her, I placed some oil in my hands and touched her forehead. The minute I laid hands on her I felt the victory. When I walked out of my mother's room my brother ask me did I want to stay awhile in the emergency waiting room. I responded "I am hungry, take me to a Chinese restaurant." When I got through eating my brother asked me did I want to go back to the hospital I responded, "no I'm sleepy take me to my uncle's house". I went to bed and slept all night without any doubt. My mother's condition changed for the better while I was sleeping. She came out of her unconsciousness I don't know if she was in coma or not, but I do know that she had been unconscious since that Friday before I got there. The next morning I got dressed for church because I believe in miracles. God had answered our families' prayer. I stopped in to see her on my way to church and my mother was sitting up eating a bowl of cream of wheat.

My home church is in Savannah, Georgia so I knew where I was going. After reading a scripture and having prayer with her that Sunday morning, I went on to church. My pastor wanted me to preach that morning. I did not mind because I was a fired up twenty–one-year-old.

When I went back to visit my mom after service, they had moved her out of the intensive care to the progressive ward. They said she was out of danger and besides that, they said she was eating too much to be a sick person.

In the mean time, my pastor asked how long I was going to be in town. I told him I had planned to stay until the following Thursday. He asked since your mother was OK, would I consider conducting a revival for three nights? I agreed, and each day I visited my mother, her condition was upgraded because she was getting stronger each day.

At the end of the revival the people were blessed and a few were added to the kingdom. My mother was also out of the hospital by the time the revival ended.

We are on the winning side. There is no reason for us to think about defeat. All power still belongs to God. Let's take our stand and reach the world for Jesus.

CONCLUSION

—⟁—

Every church (if it is of God) has its reason for existence. May you fulfill your purpose. We are here to reach the masses and not just a chosen few. This book has been produced to assist you with wisdom and knowledge that comes straight from my heart. I have been inspired by the Holy Spirit to tell it like it is.

The focus of this book stresses that there are over 6 billion people in the world. They are our harvest. May you study and utilize this material. It has not been compiled for you to take it and put it on a shelf. I deputize you to make others aware of its existence.

Pastors are under the spotlight and you must stand up and be strong. The devil is already defeated. Confront the issues in your life and get ready to experience your break-through. This comprehensive book will open your understanding like none other. If you allow the Holy Spirit, He will use you to lead your congregation into a large group of healthy believers.

The unique thing about this book is, it is easy to read and follow. It has instructions that speak directly to heart and it doesn't beat around the bush. Most of all, it gives solutions rather than attacking and insulting small churches. It teaches what to do.

You have covered a series of practical and workable guides in correcting the everyday little thing that's hindering you. Please know that reading is not enough. Keep studying until you obtain the desired results. It will give me great pleasure to know that my findings has made a difference in your ministry. Feel free to write me with your testimony or prayer request at:

Dr. Marvin Scott, Ph. D.
P. O. Box 150012
Alexandria, VA 22315
Or
www.odcministries.org

CPSIA information can be obtained
at www.ICGtesting.com
Printed in the USA
LVHW091541130921
697721LV00006B/133

9 781600 347009